MAKE PEACE OR DIE

MAKE PEACE OR DIE

A LIFE OF SERVICE, LEADERSHIP, AND NIGHTMARES

CHARLES U. DALY

HOUNDSTOOTH
PRESS

COPYRIGHT © 2020 CHARLES U. DALY

MAKE PEACE OR DIE
A Life of Service, Leadership, and Nightmares

ISBN 978-1-5445-1687-5 *Hardcover*
      978-1-5445-1686-8 *Paperback*
      978-1-5445-1685-1 *Ebook*

For Christine, the heart and soul of my life

CONTENTS

PROLOGUE 11

PART I: I WAS SUPPOSED TO BE A GENTLEMAN
SERVANTS AND A PRIVATE PLANE..............................19
THE WAITING ROOM 29
IN CASE OF NATIONAL EMERGENCY............................35
THE BOAT LEAVES WEDNESDAY 45
MY LUCKY STRIKE ARMY 55
ON POINT...73
A MEDAL AND A CRIME 83
GOOD NEWS, CHUCK WOUNDED 97

PART II: BITTER SAFETY
BETHESDA...111
THE STICKY ROAD TO THE WHITE HOUSE 119
A BORROWED UNIFORM 131
A SMALL MARGIN 141
WE DON'T DO PEARL HARBORS 157
TAPS..163
THE EYES OF TEXAS 173
BOBBY..185
FORTUNATE SON 197
HOPE AND HISTORY 209
MARY..217
THE DREAM..223
LOVE WALKED IN AND DROVE THE SHADOWS AWAY........229
FIELD WORK..233
EPILOGUE 249
ACKNOWLEDGMENTS 259
ABOUT THE AUTHORS..263

"Make peace or die!"

—MOTTO OF 1ST BATTALION, 5TH MARINES

PROLOGUE

RIDERLESS HORSES

NOVEMBER 22–24, 1963

"The New Frontier I speak of is not a set of promises—it is a set of challenges."

—PRESIDENT JOHN F. KENNEDY

The first time I was near an American president, he was in a box.

On April 14, 1945, I was eighteen years old. Outside Union Station, I watched a team of six white horses pull FDR's caisson on his final journey to the White House. I had been an American citizen for less than a decade at that point. Eighteen years later, I had a corner office in the West Wing of the White House as an aide to the first Irish American president. Less than a thousand days after I took that job, President Kennedy was on that same caisson.

★ ★ ★

Friday, November 22, 1963 was slow for President Kennedy's congressional relations staff. Most members had completed their Tuesday to Thursday workweek and were in their districts, chasing little white balls or engaged in other vertical and horizontal endeavors.

My boss, Larry O'Brien, special assistant to the president for congressional relations and personnel, was in Texas with President Kennedy, unlikely to call our four-man team for head counts or reports on congressional requests, demands, threats, and promises. Chief of Staff Kenny O'Donnell and Special Assistant to the President Dave Powers were also with Kennedy. Pierre Salinger, the White House press secretary, was over the Pacific, headed to Japan with much of the cabinet.

Ahead of me was a weekend with my wife, Mary, my sons, Michael and Douglas, and our spaniel, chugging along the chilly shores of the Chesapeake in our seven-horsepower wooden outboard. Lunch in the White House Mess was quiet. As I took my seat, a Filipino steward set down my oblong silver napkin ring, engraved with my name, two anchors, and the words "White House Mess." This is Washington's most exclusive eatery. For privacy and tradition, it is run by the Navy—hence the anchors. The Mess was reserved for select members of the president's senior staff. No guests were permitted at the round table in the corner where I was seated. There were four or five smaller tables where members of the staff could flatter the occasional guest with a meal at the White House. The atmosphere in the Mess was one of quiet, untouchable, and seemingly invincible power.

Just after 1:30 p.m., Jack McNally strode in. My first thought was that he must be delighted to be carrying some message from the Executive Office Building that would gain him entry to the Mess and perhaps wreck the weekend with tasks for one or another of us. His usual smile was absent.

"The president's been shot," he whispered.

"What?" I said.

"No!" said someone else.

"How bad?"

"I don't know."

I went down to the press office. Pierre Salinger's plane was out of touch. His number two, Mack Kilduff, was off covering the Dallas trip.

In the White House, we didn't know anything more than the Associated Press's first bulletin told us:

BULLETIN: DALLAS, NOV 22 (AP)—PRESIDENT KENNEDY WAS SHOT JUST AS HIS MOTORCADE LEFT DOWNTOWN DALLAS.

Sporadic updates followed, then the clacking of the newswire delivered the end of our world:

BULLETIN: DALLAS, NOV 22 (AP)—TWO PRIESTS STEPPED OUT OF PARKLAND HOSPITAL'S EMERGENCY WARD TODAY AND SAID PRESIDENT KENNEDY DIED OF HIS BULLET WOUNDS.

I went back upstairs and sat until dark calling home, ignoring messages, half watching the television chronicling the president's final flight to the Capitol. Not the new president. Not Lyndon Johnson. The president.

★ ★ ★

On the Sunday after the assassination, three hundred thousand people lined Pennsylvania Avenue to watch six white horses pull a caisson bearing the president's flag-draped casket from the White House to the Capitol Rotunda, where he would lie in state. It was the same caisson that had carried FDR and the Unknown Soldier.

Photo: Max Scheler.

There is a haunting photograph of the First Family following the president's casket up the Capitol steps. In the center of the image, the widowed Jacqueline is looking directly at the camera, a black mantilla on her head, a wisp of hair between her eyes. She is shouldering the despair of the whole country with the same poise that defined her public image as First Lady. Beside her, JFK Jr. is bounding up the steps with his tongue out, too young to fathom what has happened. You hope. Caroline's white-gloved hand is holding her mother's in black. In the foreground of this tableau of grief is the back of Kenny O'Donnell's head. He's looking off to the left, out of the frame, at the box containing our president. Kenny had been in the car behind Kennedy's in Dallas and blessed himself when he saw a chunk of the president's brain explode out of his skull. Opposite Kenny, that's me facing the camera: eyes on the First Family, hand on my heart. My hair is cropped short, the mark of a Marine who doesn't know what to do with the freedom to grow it out. I have on a lapel pin, the red, white, and blue vertical stripes of the Silver Star, which I had received twelve years earlier for my actions as a rifle platoon leader on the other side of the world. I had always been able to keep my memories of war at a safe distance by throwing myself into my work. I tried to stay too busy to dwell on bad memories. Working for the president was a great way to do that. As I stood on the steps that day, I thought about the killing I had done in the hills around Inje and Wonju, South Korea. I thought about the widows and bereaved mothers of men I had led to their deaths, and the Chinese and North Korean widows I created with my M1 Carbine and my orders. I saw the young faces of friends who came home in flag-draped boxes.

In his inaugural address, President Kennedy had challenged my generation to "Ask not what your country can do for you, ask what you can do for your country." Standing on those steps with my hand on my heart, I asked myself a question I would go on asking for the rest of my life: What can I do for my country *now*?

PART I

I WAS SUPPOSED TO BE A GENTLEMAN

SERVANTS AND A PRIVATE PLANE

1892–1927

"They shall not grow old, as we that are left grow old."

—LAWRENCE BINYON, "FOR THE FALLEN"

Mine is not your typical Irish immigrant's story. For one thing, my dad had use of a private airplane when I was growing up, a bulky Ford trimotor with silver skin and loud engines that scared the hell out of me. The plane and a private railcar were perks of my father's work as a top US executive of Shell Oil. Our family came to America on a boat, but it was an ocean liner, and we traveled first class.

We Anglo-Irish are best known for those who make history—like Oscar Wilde and the Duke of Wellington—and are therefore counted as Brits. Our relationship with British rule in Ireland is complex and often shameful. Although they were an instrument of British control on the island, the landed gentry also contributed to Ireland's many rebellions and the formation of the Irish Free State. Though protestants accounted for around 5 percent of the Republic of Ireland's population at the time I was born, and just over 4 percent today, we are represented by one-third of the tricolor flag, the orange part, with green for the Catholics and white for peace between the two. Until recently, peace was just a hope.

★ ★ ★

In 1892, my father was born in China, the son of Dr. Charles Calthrop de Burgh Daly, who set up a clinic in Ningbo following several voyages to China as a ship's doctor. It seems he found the human suffering in that ancient kingdom too hard to ignore. He stayed and married Emily French, an Irish nurse with similar ideals who was also the sister of Irish songwriter and poet Percy French.

My Aunt Lucy tells how my grandfather's hospital came to be in a letter:

> In 1893, he moved to Yingkwo, N. Manchuria just before the Chinese-Japanese war broke out. He was the first person to start Red Cross work for the Chinese; up to then their wounded were just left to die... The Dowager Empress of China decorated him with the Order of the Double Dragon. He also received a wooden plaque in a beautifully carved frame inscribed in Chinese characters:

> In difficulty and danger, you helped us.

> ...in 1911, when we were home on leave in Dublin, bubonic plague broke out in Manchuria. A colleague cabled:

> For God's sake come to me, Daly, we are dying.

He was also decorated by the British, Russian, and Japanese governments for his work. Our family's time in China is recorded by my grandmother, Emily Lucy de Burgh Daly, in her travelogue,

An Irishwoman in China, which her brother, whom she refers to by his full name, Mr. Percy French, helped edit. She documents my grandfather's work and her own, running a women's clinic. They met professionally, and in her memoirs, she always refers to him as "Dr. Daly," and in true Anglo fashion, she leaves out even a hint of romance.

Dr. Daly introduced provincial China to the miracle of cataract surgery. My Aunt Lucy relates the effect of this procedure:

> "A person went into the hospital blind and came out seeing! 'Hai-yah! these *yiang-kne-tze* (foreign devils) *do* know a thing or two!'"

Their son, my father, was shipped home to be educated at the prestigious and brutal Tonbridge School and went on to Cambridge, where he graduated in the doomed class of 1914.

★ ★ ★

Ironically, it was war weariness that prompted Dr. Daly to return to Ireland in 1913, leaving the rebellions in China the year before the Western world went mad.

My father (far left) and uncle (to the right of my father) and everyone in this photo was killed or wounded.

I keep a photo of my father taken during the First World War. In it, my dad stands in his officer's uniform with binoculars and a walking stick. Beside him, my mother's nineteen-year-old brother, Charlie, a lieutenant, leans on his rifle in a confident pose, half smiling behind his pipe. They are flanked by a few others. One is wearing a German army helmet with the spike on top, a war trophy.

What war does to men can be detected in the difference between their expressions. My dad has the proverbial thousand-yard stare. The corners of his eyes around his spectacles and his brows show resignation and an exhausted readiness. The men under his command have a similar look. Charlie, on the other hand, has the fresh face of a replacement, a gentleman for whom war is still a great adventure. Charlie has only been on the front for less than a week. He would be killed shortly after this photo was taken.

My dad handed down this photo to me and scribbled the names of the men under it with "KIA" or "WIA" beside each name, marking them all killed or wounded. I thought of cropping the photo to make it a family shot, and I'm glad I didn't. Those guys had already been cropped out.

Shortly after my own war, I asked Dad, "When do the bad memories fade?"

"It will take a long, long time, but finally they will fade."

As of today, mine have not.

★ ★ ★

Dad had gone to the front in the 4th battalion of the Royal Dublin Fusiliers, having applied for a commission on the day war broke out. He was made a captain following a perfunctory officer's training course. While his sons were at war, my grandfather managed two hospitals in Ireland that handled the overflow of wounded. In 1917, he was awarded an Order of the British Empire for this work. My uncle, Lieutenant Arthur Charles de Burgh Daly, another Charlie, was killed in action on September 9, 1916, after having seen action and survived in the Somme. He was nineteen years old. In his last letter home, he wrote,

> "We attack Grinchy tomorrow. In case of accidents, I played the game two days ago, and will, please God, tomorrow."

The next morning, he led his men over the top and was hit in the ear with a bit of shrapnel. He took cover in a shell crater to assess the wound and regain his composure. According to the official report, he stood up, made it four or five yards toward the enemy wire before having his head shattered by machine-gun fire. Due to a cruel administrative error, my family would receive word that he had been wounded, then they were told that report was an error and that Charlie was fine. Finally, they learned the truth, or a polite version of the truth.

Aunt Lucy joined the war as a nurse's aide in a Volunteer Aide Detachment (V.A.D.) after losing both her brother and the love of her life in France. She never married but lived a full and adventurous life, seeing the world as a solitary traveler.

Dad was wounded in the left thigh and right hand at Richebourg–L'Avoue on May 9, 1915. While convalescing in Dublin, he, like many other Irish soldiers in British uniform, played a role in putting down the 1916 Easter Rising that I'm glad I don't know much about. Shortly after his return to the front as a major, in June 1916, he was sent home again, with appendicitis, and spent the rest of the war training "bombers" in the art of grenade throwing. For his wounds, he was given a lump sum, or "blood money" as he called it, which he spent on a motorbike. After the armistice, he putt-putted around Ireland on the bike for several months visiting the families of young officers who had been killed while serving under his command. He eased painful memories by describing deaths courageous and quick even in cases where the truth was pathetic and grotesque.

Dad's jaunts by bike and train around Ireland led him up the winding drive of Richmount, a semi-grand residence in Bandon, where he met the parents and sister of Lt. Charles Sealy King, the man beside him in the photo who, like his own brother Charles, had been killed while attempting to lead an Irish platoon into machine guns and barbed wire.

Lt. King's surviving sister, Violet, became his wife and my mother.

Dad on the motorcycle he bought with the payout for his wounds.

Violet Sealy King impressed my father with her independence. She had reacted to her brother Charles's death by leaving County Cork for the first time in her life to volunteer as a V.A.D in a hospital behind the lines in France and in the slaughter at Gallipoli. Violet left behind a life of lunches, lawn games, picnics, tennis, bridge, and ping-pong. Mum never spoke about her service, but when it came my turn to go to war, she had no illusions about what her son would experience. Later, she told me she had little hope of seeing me again.

After my father finished his tour of Ireland, which included three return visits to Richmount, he went to London in search of work. He and "Vi" kept up a correspondence. In her 1919 diary, she writes of his visits to Bandon. First calling him "Major D." and later "Himself." He picked a lily of the valley for her.

Dad got a job at the London office of Royal Dutch Shell (just "Shell" today), where he found row on row of desks filled with other survivors of a decimated generation. Discussing this gloomy scene with a bored interviewer, he learned there was one unwanted job open—peddling Shell Oil products in rural India. He seized the chance. Within a month, he embarked on a sweltering passage by way of the Mediterranean and the Suez Canal, happy to be sailing away from clerkdom and bad memories.

His base was Malabar, a minor town 150 miles south of Bombay. There he lived the life of a midlevel Raj until, less than a year after his arrival, Dad found himself in the midst of yet another bloodbath that would once again change his destiny. Although a civilian, Dad lent his assistance to the military force that put down the 1921 Moplah Rising, drawing upon his wartime experience to defend British and Hindu lives and property from the Islamic rebels who were killing, raping, and forcibly converting their "infidel" neighbors. Dad organized a little convoy of open cars and bicycles to rescue an isolated group under siege in a village. Captain McEnroy, of the local garrison, wrote a note to Shell, saying that my father "set an example of coolness and gallantry worthy of the best traditions of the service."

Amid the chaos, my father wrote to Violet and proposed marriage. She then traveled to India at a time when such passages had become known as the "fishing fleet," packed with women, ostensibly on holidays or seeking work, but actually looking to land a mate from the survivors of the war. In later years, Mum liked to remind us that *she* was different from her shipmates because she was sailing toward an altar where she would kneel on a date certain. They were married on November 9, 1921. Before leaving India, they had a daughter, Joan.

I was born on May 29, 1927, shortly after their return to Ireland.

Thanks to Dad's heroics in the Moplah Rising and as a consequence of an earthquake in Japan that killed a number of Shell executives, he soon found himself fast-tracked to the highest levels of the company, first cleaning up the mess in Japan, and then on to the senior position in America that included a private plane and railcar.

THE WAITING ROOM

1930–1945

"Look at the way Americans work, even on a Sunday."

—ULICK DE BURGH DALY, MY FATHER

In St. Louis, my father, Ulick, became "Mike," my sister, Ann, was born, the first American in our family, and I saw my first baseball game. Of all the perks that came with Dad's work at Shell—the plane, the railcar, the drivers, and lakeshore holidays in Michigan—the one that most interested me were Cardinals tickets to Sportsman's Park. Dad took me to our first game. I remember him taking it all in. Maybe he had heard something about "three strikes and you're out," or maybe he understood the game the way many Brits do as just like rounders. One of us would come away from that first game a lifelong Cardinals fan, of the legendary "Gashouse Gang"—Frankie Frisch, Joe Medwick, the Dean Brothers, Rip Collins, Leo Durocher, et al. I was captivated by the beautiful ballpark, the noise, the cheers, and the peanuts. Most of all, I remember being in the stands with my father. I don't remember a single play or the outcome of any of the games. But I remember spending time with him.

Until World War II broke out in 1939, there were summer crossings to Ireland. I was a brat with the run of first class and my own private steward. During those Irish summers, I spent much of my time under the influence of Aunt Lucy, the vagabond bachelorette. My sister, Joan, claims that's where I got my adventuresome streak.

Richmond was a fifty-acre estate with fields running down to the River Bandon. There were no other children around, but my sisters and I found ways to amuse ourselves. Electricity was spotty to nonexistent, but it was light enough to play outside 'til 10:00 p.m., or even later, in the summers. In those days, the baker still made our home deliveries by horse and cart.

The Great Depression ended the good times at Shell. Ours became a more modest life. Ever the adventurer and optimist, dad wildcatted for oil in Michigan, and came up dry. He started a water softener company and became secretary treasurer of a manufacturing firm that needed honest management. Prohibition was one American cultural practice that my parents could not accept. They were appalled by America's puritanical attitudes about liquor and employed a bootlegger who made sure they would never want for their evening martinis.

It wasn't long before war caught up with the Dalys once again. In 1940, despairing of America's neutrality up until that point, dad tried to enlist in the British Army despite his age and wounds from the last war. It outraged him to be turned away. I remember his ire and his low opinion of the ragtag Home Guard that Churchill was assembling to "fight on the beaches and in the streets."

Dad would say, "I could instruct the Home Guard, they know nothing." He would recite a poem to that point:

Home Guard Harry got his gun,

Loaded it and shot his son.

"My," said Harry, "Ain't that good,

it works just like they said it would."

As a poor second to directly fighting Hitler, he secured a post at the British embassy in Washington running key parts of Lend-Leasing, a purchasing operation FDR had developed to lend ships and munitions to England in exchange for base leases and promises. The same U-boats that threatened to strangle Britain's shipping also prevented us from returning to Ireland during wartime summers. My father was awarded an Order of the British Empire (OBE) for his work in Lend-Leasing.

During the war, we lived in a small rented brick home on Cheltenham Drive in Bethesda. We ate roast beef dinners and went on short weekend drives—ever mindful of the gas gauge.

I will not forget one drive into Washington on a particularly balmy winter Sunday. As we were cruising down Constitution Avenue in our old Ford, my father pointed out all the civil servants rushing into the Navy Department building:

"Look at the way Americans work, even on a Sunday."

Back home, we turned on the radio and learned what all the commotion was about. It was Sunday, December 7, 1941. The Japanese had just bombed Pearl Harbor.

★ ★ ★

One day in early 1942, Dad invited me to go on a drive to Baltimore, where he had a doctor's appointment. He'd been having difficulty with his balance. I wasn't worried. For me, it was a day off from school, a whole day alone with Dad. As usual, he didn't speak much, but I was so happy just riding along, smelling the smoke from his pipe, silently admiring him in his tweed suit, his steel-rimmed glasses, his mustache, and as always the rosebud Mum put in his lapel every spring morning. He was so big and so strong; at least that's how I remember him.

Listening outside a half-open door at Johns Hopkins Hospital, I heard words I half understood:

> "I think we've found the difficulty. It's serious. You may have multiple sclerosis. There's not much to be done, but you should live for some years if you take care of yourself. No smoking, no alcohol, and there won't be much more golf."

> After a heavy silence, my father replied, "Do you want me to live in a vacuum tube? Good day, Doctor."

Joining me in the waiting room, he said, "Charlie, say goodbye to the doctor. We must get home in time to have tonight's martini with Mum."

The drive home was long. How could my mighty father be dealt such a rotten hand? Not a curse or a whine from him, not then nor once through all the years of physical decline. My father's best hope in fighting the disease was his own strength of will. As his symptoms worsened, he could have taken to a wheelchair, but he opted for the strenuous alternative: a pair of canes. He kept on working.

I plodded through Bethesda Chevy Chase High School with what was at best a mediocre academic record and eased the boredom of school by holding odd jobs. In the spring of 1945, I joined the Navy. For my parents, this may have been confirmation of our fall from gentility: their only son was going to war as an enlisted man.

IN CASE OF NATIONAL EMERGENCY

1945–1950

"No man in my family has failed officer training."

—VIOLET DE BURGH DALY, MY MOTHER

Much of the good in my life from this point forward I owe to a single piece of legislation: the G.I. Bill. But before I could reap the benefits of my adoptive country's most generous moment, or reflect on the politics of it, there were latrines to scrub, gangplanks to guard, and decks to swab.

Navy boot camp in Bainbridge, Maryland, started badly. Upon arrival, we recruits were tossed uniforms, shorn of hair, and handed cups of coffee. My first cup ever. I vomited onto my hands, rubbed them dry on the soles of my shoes. I have never had another cup.

Boot camp was dull and technical. The high point was firefighting school. In a mock aircraft carrier hangar, we learned the deadly reason one doesn't spray water on a gasoline fire directly and how to smother the flames with a mist instead. We were trained in the use of radios and telephones. The headsets frightened some of the country kids who couldn't believe it possible to hear the voice of someone who wasn't in the room.

To get out of compulsory Sunday church services, I claimed I was Jewish. For this I was assigned punitive cleaning duties, scrubbing latrines. Whether this was because of anti-Semitism or because the Navy doesn't like liars or both, I will never know.

All recruits were compelled to box. My sparring partner was a brute who had fun beating the living crap out of me. I was saved by Ira Cohen, genuinely Jewish, who offered to switch sparring partners. He proceeded to savagely beat the guy who'd been doing a job on me.

I became interested in anything that paid more than "twenty-one dollars a day, once a month." At first, I thought of volunteering as a submariner. The cramped sunless and unsafe life aboard a sub came with a significant bump over base pay and a bit of prestige and adventure. There were no openings. My big break was the V-5 program that had been set up to train naval aviators. This included a full ride at university and commission as an officer. CPO (Chief Petty Officer, aka God) Korowski was required to inform all men under his command about this unbelievable opportunity. On a good day, he was a mean son of a bitch. He assembled my fellow shipmates and me at attention and asked if any of us wanted to volunteer for V-5. A dozen of us stepped forward.

"I told you cock sucking miserable mother fucking sons of two-bit whores never to volunteer for anything I didn't volunteer you for!"

CPO Korowski couldn't keep us from applying, but he could make our lives hell until we got our orders or were turned down for the program. He had us clean latrines, remove yards of rust with dull scrapers, polish floors, haul garbage, and clean more latrines.

The V-5 candidates were pruned out based on intelligence and aptitude tests we had taken when we enlisted. Those of us who qualified for the next step faced a board of officers with additional questions. I got that far. One question stands out in my memory:

"Give an example of one of Newton's three laws of motion."

By some miracle, I had retained something about "an equal but opposite reaction" from Chevy Chase High School. After that, the rest of the screening was a character assessment—questions about sports and current events, to see if I was the sort of guy who belonged in the fraternity of the air. One officer wanted to know why I chose the Navy over the Army Air Corps if I'm so interested in flying. I piously answered, "Sir, I don't want to be a flying soldier. I love the Navy."

I passed.

Korowski broke the news: "Daly, you can get your head out of the shitcan now. Here are your orders. You are going to fucking college. You have been fucking useless here, so maybe they'll teach you to fly around a classroom. Good luck and goodbye."

CPO Korowski even shook my hand. I was college bound, but I didn't know which college, nor did I care. Those of us who had passed the test were assembled from our various East Coast stations. At muster, role was called: Daly, Davis, Loftis, Munroe: to New Haven, Connecticut. Yale University.

The others, with the last names "N" through "Z," were sent to Schenectady, New York: Union College.

* * *

At Yale we wore uniforms, drilled, and held empty rifles while we guarded our college gates as we gazed upon our white-shoed betters headed for frat parties and similar joys. Our uniforms were a constant reminder that we were in the Navy and not true men of Yale.

The war had ended not long after I joined the Navy. The Japanese must have known I was coming. After my freshman year at Yale, the aviation cadet program was dissolved. I could stay on at Yale but had to sign a seven-year contract. No way. I wouldn't sign, so I was sent to Norfolk, still a Seaman Second Class, to guard a gangplank. Fortunately, the peacetime Navy didn't need me for long. I received an honorable discharge on August 21, 1946.

* * *

To my stunned delight, I found that I still had some more American generosity coming my way. Thanks to the G.I. Bill, I was entitled to a year for having enlisted and one additional day of college for every day I had served, including my time in uniform at Yale. That was just enough to complete my studies and earn a bachelor's degree. To top off this bonanza, Yale welcomed me back in September as a regular student in regular clothes, free to study whatever I wanted. I chose international relations.

During my marvelous sophomore year, I belatedly discovered women. My sexual education, to that point, had been nonexistent. Even my fantasies had been vague. I made up for lost time, hitting the town with a fellow G.I. Bill recipient, T. George Harris, who would become a lifelong friend. He was a veteran of the Battle of the Bulge and would go on to found *Psychology Today* magazine. I would meet two extraordinary professors who would make me excited about learning for its own sake. Andrew Georgy came from Eastern Europe and taught history. I was impressed by his intellect and by his past service as an infantryman with a PhD. Professor Kennedy called Yale "this place" and seemed to sense my own restlessness and lack of belonging.

For spending money, I worked afternoons in a laundromat and as a night watchman in the Peabody Museum of Natural History.

★ ★ ★

In the summer of 1947, I went hitchhiking around the country. At my elder sister Joan's suggestion, I dropped in on her in-laws in Chicago. They took me to Lake Geneva, Wisconsin, for a weekend at their cottage. We went to the Belfry Summer Playhouse to see *Another Part of the Forest*. I was so stunned by one of the performers that I stayed at the lake for three days trying, without success, to seduce the star, Mary Larmonth. I was overdue to meet my high school friend, Bob Wallace, in St. Louis, so reluctantly, I left. Bob and I had a rough trip hitchhiking to Mexico City. By car and finally via a two-dollar bus ride from Laredo, we found ourselves drinking beer on a punt through the floating gardens of Xochimilco. Bedeviled by endless hangovers and almost broke, we hitchhiked our way over the long, hot roads home.

On the road, 1947.

Back at Yale for my junior year, I was bored despite good friends and touch football games. I couldn't get Mary out of my mind. I invited her to spend Thanksgiving with me at my parents' home in Bethesda. We rented a canoe on the Potomac, where we spent an unforgettable moonlit night on rocky little Roosevelt Island. After that, there were many hitchhiking trips to Chicago, where Mary was working in Demmet's candy store by day and doing theater at night. Finally, she decided to move to New York where Norm, her Canadian father, used his clout as an Episcopal priest to get her into a fancy but overly sheltered rooming house on Gramercy Park. I would visit from New Haven, and we'd get a ten-dollar per night room at the Chesterfield on Fifty-Second Street and eat five-dollar boiled dinners for two on Eighth Avenue.

★ ★ ★

At some point, I got to thinking that all of this was one hell of a deal for an immigrant. I couldn't get over the idea that I owed my country everything. I was possessed by the restless and romantic feeling that I ought to pay my country back through further service. At Yale, I heard of a Marine Corps program that would make me a commissioned officer if I spent the summer between my junior and senior years getting paid to train in Quantico, Virginia. My sister Joan's husband, John, had been a WWII Marine in the Pacific. The qualities I recognized and admired in John were almost nonexistent among my classmates. I'm talking about that "the few, the proud" stuff that has led many good men to early deaths and others to disillusionment and boredom in a branch of the service affectionately nicknamed "the suck." A brotherhood, in any case.

After a six-week summer camp, I was a Marine officer. The official name for this perfunctory officer's school was Platoon Leaders Class (PLC), but among the more experienced senior enlisted, the men who actually ran the Marine Corps, PLC was known as "Prick's Last Chance." I was commissioned a second lieutenant in the peacetime Marine Corps. Dad didn't have much to say about it, perhaps because he knew peace seldom lasts.

As a Marine reservist, my standby orders read something like: *Only to be called upon in case of national emergency.*

Mary and I got married on a Saturday. I got to work on Monday.

Instead of attending graduation, Mary and I got married on a Saturday, and we both went to work on Monday. She worked at a department store, and I got a job unloading millions of gallons of industrial molasses from ocean-going tankers at a pier in Baltimore for a British company.

My staff consisted of one man: Nelson Parker, who could have run the place if he hadn't been born with black skin. He was a hard worker, but I noticed that he would disappear a couple of times a day for twenty or thirty minutes.

"Nelson, I don't mind you taking a break, but where do you go?"

"To the toilet."

"What's the matter with the toilet in the office?"

"That's for white folks."

"*What?*"

My predecessor had abided by and apparently agreed with a practice that segregated even two men. Nelson had walked, rain or shine, a quarter mile to a "colored" toilet in a nearby railroad yard. That idiotic policy ended as soon as I became aware of it.

Nelson used to fish for crabs by the pier for dinner. His girlfriend was blind, and he would read to her from the Encyclopedia Britannica. Much of his life was unknown to me as we lived on opposite sides of that ugly color divide, but we managed to strike up a friendship of sorts, bonding over the monotony of waiting for molasses tankers.

Nelson Parker, molasses tanks in the background.

Mary and I were earning enough to buy a car and rent a little house on Chesapeake Bay. We were so happy.

THE BOAT LEAVES WEDNESDAY

JUNE 1950–FEBRUARY 1951

"In war, as in prostitution, amateurs are often better than professionals."

—NAPOLEON BONAPARTE

On June 25, 1950, we got our national emergency.

At dawn that morning, the (North) Korean People's Army surged over the 38th parallel into the South. This action was immediately condemned by an emergency session of the UN Security Council, a vote from which the Soviets abstained.

The Korean peninsula had been divided since the end of World War II under an agreement between the US and USSR with no consideration of the will of the Korean people. Before that, from 1910–1945, Korea was a colony of the Japanese Empire and suffered unimaginable atrocities ranging from forced labor and sex slavery to medical experimentation on human subjects. After World War II, North Korea was run by Kim Il Sung, who had been a charismatic resistance fighter during Japanese occupation. He used Soviet and Chinese subsidies to model a state on Stalin's Russia, labor camps and all. The South, no bastion of democracy, was run by a corrupt and brutal puppet government that took

America's backing as license to pillage and deprive its people and massacre political opponents. The United States had adopted an official noninterference policy that gave the North reason to believe their invasion would be uncontested by South Korea's mightiest ally.[1]

On June 30, five days after the North's invasion of the South began, Truman sent American troops to support the South Koreans. On July 7, the UN passed Resolution 84, requesting member nations to join a "police action" on the Korean peninsula. Sixteen nations joined in, including ones with modest armies like Ethiopia and Turkey. General MacArthur, who had been serving as de facto emperor of Japan since the war's end, was given command of UN forces. Unfortunately for the South Koreans, MacArthur's army of the occupation were not the same men who won the Second World War. Many were drunk and fat from half a decade of soft living as occupiers. In Korea, they were beaten back, almost off the peninsula, by Kim Il-Sung's peasant fighters, making their last stand outside the port of Pusan. The outcome looked bleak.

On September 15, MacArthur ordered the Marines under his command to make an amphibious landing at the port of Incheon, near Seoul. The plan was to retake the capital and cut across the middle of the peninsula, thus trapping all North Korean troops in the south and taking the pressure off Pusan. It worked. The Communist invaders were killed, captured, or pushed back over the original border.

Roughly two weeks after the Incheon landing, Chinese Premier Zhou Enlai had warned that China would intervene if American and other UN troops moved north of the 38th parallel. On

---

1   David Douglas Duncan, *This is War! A Photo-Narrative of the Korean War.*

October 7, MacArthur ordered his forces to do just that. China soon began secretly sending "volunteers" into North Korea and strengthening their own border defenses along the Yalu River. Around the same time, MacArthur met with President Truman and assured him that the Chinese would not intervene.

Mary and I knew little of Korea's history. Neither of us knew or cared about America's blundered diplomacy and intelligence failures that had left Korea in a national security blind spot. Our interest increased sharply when North Korea invaded the South. Mary's attention skyrocketed when I reminded her of my standby orders and speculated that this skirmish qualified as a national emergency. My call to duty came shortly after Truman committed troops to the UN's response to North Korea's assault. I went to our local post office where a Navy corpsman was giving the Marine physicals. I've always had low blood pressure. When the doc double-checked it, he wanted to turn me away. I had already taken leave from work and had gotten excited about going to war. I told him I'd be right back, went and ran up and down a few flights of stairs, and returned somewhat breathless for a re-exam. The corpsman said something to the effect of, "Hey pal, if you're dumb enough to go, I'm dumb enough to send you."

While I checked into Quantico, Mary found a cabin with a wood-burning stove in the pines near Lake Jackson, an elongated puddle at the western edge of the vast Marine base. By day and night, our new nest was often rocked by explosions from the artillery range. The sounds of freedom disturbed Mary, but we enjoyed the seclusion. On chilly autumn nights, when training didn't have me fumbling around land navigation courses in the dark woods, I would sit by the fire or lie in bed with Mary and talk dreams about the arrival of our baby. Unspoken was the consolation that she was pregnant and would at least have our child in the event that my absence became permanent.

Up until that point, my military training had consisted of PLC, that summer camp at Quantico in 1948. Before deploying to Korea, I would receive additional training in the first-ever class of the Special Basic School. Those eleven weeks were consumed by seasoned Marines vainly trying to teach Second Lieutenant Daly to read maps and lead riflemen. Not that I was going to need any of the skills I was learning; it looked as though the war would be over before we got our platoons.

In early November 1950, MacArthur ordered a drive all the way up to the Chinese border. He made the infamous promise that his victorious troops would be home for Christmas. All the Dalys were happy to hear this news. At this point, I was still at Quantico, and it looked as though the war would end before my classmates and I deployed. Then, on November 26, the Chinese launched an immense surprise attack, routing all UN forces from coast to coast and trapping the US Marines at the Chosin Reservoir, outnumbering them by upwards of four-to-one. The action that followed became known as "Frozen Chosin." The Marines held their positions with little support, totally cut off from the unprotected supply lines that MacArthur had stretched thin behind them. They fought in near-arctic conditions. Their canned rations froze. Their weapons froze. Their limbs froze. Men froze to death. In some instances, frozen enemy dead were stacked in front of Marine fighting positions and used as sandbags.

Needless to say, any Marine who survived Chosin became legend. It borders on absurd to think that I, a twenty-three-year-old lieutenant, would soon be giving orders to men who had fought their way out of that cold hell. One such man I would go on to command was Gunther Dohse, a German immigrant who was one of just sixteen men in a rifle company of 200-plus to walk out of Chosin, already a recipient of the Silver Star and Purple Heart when I met him.

★ ★ ★

After training, each Marine is assigned an MOS, or Military Occupational Specialty. The MOS for an infantry officer is 0301. After Chosin, we at the Basic School took to calling it 03-oh-shit! By year's end, 1950, the situation in Korea was so grim that Truman was seriously considering removing all US forces from the peninsula. By New Year's 1951, the second wave of the Chinese offensive had pushed the UN coalition south of the 38th parallel, forcing them to surrender Seoul for the second time. My Special Basic Class graduated around the time the Division broke out from their encirclement at Chosin. It was one of the Corps' finest hours. But for us, it meant the war was just getting started. We had to fill out requests for next duty assignments. Most of us would be given orders to Korea, but most made their first choice something other than infantry. Only five lieutenants in my training company requested to lead a rifle platoon, and I was one of them. My orders were to report to Camp Pendleton, near San Diego, California, before shipping out across the Pacific.

I said goodbye to my parents in Bethesda. Dad gave me a .45 caliber Smith & Wesson revolver, saying that a personal weapon had been of comfort in the trenches.

He kissed me goodbye and hugged me. I can't recall him doing either before. The family's war history must have been on his mind as it was on mine. All through my deployment, my mother would garden nervously and dig holes in the yard.

Mary and I planned to drive west in our 1949 Ford, but Mary was having trouble riding with the pregnancy, so she followed by train.

Rents were high in California, but a Basic School classmate, Angus Deming, and I found a house near the beach in Carlsbad. After moving into what would have been a dream home in other circumstances, Angus and I drove north to Camp Pendleton. Checking in, I explained to the weathered sergeant on duty that we had just arrived and gave the young wives' bit and asked for an added week's leave.

"The boat leaves Diego on Wednesday."

Angus and I decided to break the news separately and gently to our wives. The moment I walked in the door, Mary looked at my face and started to cry. Angus's bride heard the news through the bathroom door. She screamed.

Mary and I spent Sunday night in a hotel in LA where she would catch the train back East. Saying goodbye was too painful, so I joked nervously as I was about to head for the elevator, "I'll be back unless I lose these," and gestured to what Marines call "the brains."

"Come back. Just come back."

Taking one last look up toward our hotel room, I saw Mary let two rolls of toilet paper stream out the window.

Bon voyage.

She sold the car, packed, and set out on a lonely transcontinental train ride to a modest apartment just outside of DC. It's a good thing she didn't stay with the other Marine wives, because too many became widows.

★ ★ ★

At muster on Monday, I was given responsibility for thirty or so enlisted Marines in the Fifth Replacement Draft. The draft's mission was to bring the depleted Marine forces on the Korean peninsula back up to strength for a counteroffensive.

As I inspected their weapons and gear, the platoon sergeant advised me that many of these boys were virgins and suggested we rectify that before heading out. That night, a dozen of us crossed the US/Mexico border and, with the help of the sergeant, found a Tijuana brothel, *El Serape*, where I negotiated a group rate, using my best college Spanish and some gestures to explain to the ladies it wouldn't take these lads long. Not only was I the officer in charge of these guys but at twenty-three, I was older than almost all of them. This was not lost on our hosts, who called these Marines *niños* (boys).

On our way out, the ladies gathered to bid us farewell, offering streamers and feigned tears.

Years later, I was at a hotel bar in Veracruz, Mexico. I kept getting looks from one of the barmen. Finally, he shouted out *"El Serape!"* where he had been working when I came in on my way to war.

★ ★ ★

Dockside Wednesday morning, I bought $10,000 worth of short-term life insurance from an enterprising Aetna Life salesman, supplementing the government's policy of the same amount. I would be taking over a platoon where most, if not all, of my predecessors had been killed or wounded. If I thought about it, I was fucked. But I didn't think about it.

For the next two weeks, the seventy-one junior officers and 1,717 enlisted Marines sailed west aboard the USS *General JC Breckinridge*. We lieutenants played a lot of poker and led calisthenic workouts on deck. At the international dateline, first-time crossers had to run the gauntlet of enlisted men slapping us silly, per tradition. We made a stop in Yokosuka, Japan, for two days, picking up supplies and ammunition. We had a chance to call home. There was a long line to use the phones, it was crowded, and I couldn't hear well.

In a room full of Marines, I shouted a crude farewell into the receiver to Mary, "You bet your sweet ass I love you."

The first Marines off the ship had managed to get drunk and in trouble before the rest of us could even get down the gangplank. We were ordered to remain on the base, officers included. Eager to experience the finer points of Japanese culture, I assembled a squad of likeminded Marines, lined them up in formation, and marched them to the main gate, sternly bringing the ranks to a halt. I told the sentry that we were under orders to move into town and round up our misbehaving comrades. Outside the gate, I told the men to scatter, have fun, fuck their brains out, drink themselves stupid, but don't get arrested, and do not miss the ship. I was showered with words of gratitude and promises to return on time. A fellow Basic School graduate, Pete McCloskey, whom I had met on the troop ship, made it ashore earlier. I found him in a geisha house infested with officers based in Japan. At one point, a Navy officer came from another room and pompously ordered us to quiet down. When he returned to his party, I threw an empty bottle through the paper screen wall, apparently striking someone. We heard a yell and then sirens. Pete and I clambered through a skylight and spent the night bivouacked on the roof. In the morning, everyone made it back to the ship. However just before departure, six officers were ordered to stay in Japan. One was the future evangelist and presidential candidate, Pat Robertson. Pat got his daddy—then United States Senator A. Willis Robertson—to have him pulled off the ship, because Pat was probably having second thoughts about dying for his country. The other five lieutenants were pulled, possibly to cover for Pat's preferential treatment.

We landed at Pohang, a port on the east coast of Korea. An announcement from the captain came over the ship's PA: "The United States Navy wishes all departing Marines good luck."

"Ten dollars to the man who shoots that silly bastard," came a shout from Sergeant "Muzzle Blast" Baker, known for a voice so loud it could drown out gunfire.

We were taken ashore by LST landing craft operated under contract by the Japanese, now our allies. I remember one Marine sizing up our diminutive skipper, "Who won the fucking war?"

From Pohang we were driven up into the hills in the back of trucks. The road was rough, the benches hard and cold. Nobody spoke. I thought about Mary and felt alone. It could be that this was one of my most frightening memories of the war. The men to my left and to my right were still strangers, and we had not yet encountered the action that would bond us and give us the courage to get through much darker nights.

At one piss stop we heard that we had already lost some guys from another convoy, not slain in some glorious fight, but squashed by their vehicle when it skidded off the rutted road and rolled down the steep hillside.

One lieutenant of our group, O'Shea, was a bachelor who counted on his pay accumulating during his deployment, but he had gambled accordingly in poker games on the ship to Korea by trying to fill inside straights and other optimistic bets. It has been said, "If you want to hear God laugh, tell him your plans for tomorrow." Others have said, "No plan survives first contact with the enemy." In O'Shea's first contact with the enemy, he got his nose shot off. He was shipped home with no money and no nose.

We reached 1st Division's 5th Marine Regiment at the front, not a line of trenches, just some high hills, narrow valleys, and a small river with enemy lurking in the long night. Pete McCloskey and I were assigned to Charlie Company, 1st Battalion. The motto of 1st Battalion, 5th Marines is "Make peace or die." For those of us who had just arrived in Korea, the latter seemed much more likely.

MY LUCKY STRIKE ARMY

FEBRUARY–MAY 1951

"You smug-faced crowds who watch with kindling eye
and cheer as soldier lads march by,
sneak home and pray you'll never know
the hell where youth and laughter go."

—SIEGFRIED SASSOON, "A SUICIDE IN THE TRENCHES"

Before the Corps could assign me a rifle platoon to command, I was designated the battalion's supply officer. A lieutenant would have to be killed, wounded, or least likely of all, rotated home before I got a platoon. This assignment put me in charge of the battalion's ammunition, supplies, and around fifty Korean laborers known as "chiggy bearers." A *chigae* is a wooden A-frame pack used by rural Koreans to carry immense loads on their backs. Our chiggy bearers carried food, water, supplies, and ammo up steep hills and carried wounded and dead down, thus making it possible to keep frontline Marines and soldiers supplied deep in the roadless terrain. This was unglamorous, sometimes fatal work for which these men were underpaid and undecorated. They were small in stature, men and boys who were too old, too young, or otherwise unfit for military service. They had no weapons, no rain gear, no sleeping bags, or tents. Many of them walked in mud, slush, and snow in makeshift sandals fashioned from wood or old tires. They would break their backs for extra American cigarettes, they would walk unarmed into gunfire to carry our wounded out. We called them "gooks," just like our enemy. Unable to tell these men how much I admired their courage and pitied their circumstances, I scrounged extra food, extra Lucky Strike cigarettes, torn or bloodied jackets, worn-out boots, and millions of Korean won, paper money that was almost worthless. I squatted with them by their fires, exchanging jokes by signs and gestures, sharing gooey canned rations and their garlic rice. Sometimes, I was able to get a Navy corpsman to treat their wounds and illnesses and, above all, their feet.

One of my favorite chiggies was a bewhiskered guy with a grand total of four or five tobacco-stained teeth. One day, speaking through our interpreter, my guy begged to be given leave to return home to visit his supposedly dying wife. How he got word of his wife's condition inside our tight world, I know not. There were no doubt line-crossers among the men, but this guy had earlier demonstrated brass balls. I wrote him a pass and had the battalion translator instruct him to hand it to any American units he met along the way:

> This man is a stretcher bearer for Charlie Company, 1st Battalion, 5th Marines. He has saved Marine lives. He is returning to Wonju on emergency leave.

> If he is found anywhere off the line between Inje and Wonju, or if he presents this pass after the date on the reverse side, kill him.
>
> —2ND LT. CHARLES U. DALY, C.O. KOREAN
> LABOR BATTALION, 5TH MARINES

He got back to us a couple of days later. I recovered the pass, grateful we hadn't changed positions in his absence.

The chiggy bearers didn't have helmets, so I didn't wear mine when I was with them. Besides the weight and discomfort, I felt that to wear it was poor leadership in that situation. The Corps had taught me to never take anything that my men couldn't have. How was I supposed to earn their respect and lead the chiggies if I ordered them to enter the fight with rags on their heads while I protected my white skull, and the precious Ivy League thoughts it contained, with American steel? The command didn't see it my way. First the battalion commander, Colonel Hopkins, ordered me not to squat with the peasants, saying it was conduct unbecoming an officer. Having given that a nod but taking no action, I was further reprimanded by a cleanly dressed major visiting from regiment.

He spoke with a lisp that had earned him the nickname Elmer Fudd, "Lieutenant *Dawey*, if you don't stop *sweawing* and start *weawing* your *helmwet*, I will have you *twansfwewed* out of this *battawion*."

Marines have a slur for these scrubbed, disciplined, rear echelon types. We call them POGs, Persons Other than Grunts. One early spring morning, when we were in the rear, I saw this distinction boil over and nearly turn deadly. Four chiggies, including the widower, were carrying a gut-shot North Korean who had been hit during a minor skirmish the night before and had been found aimlessly crawling on the hill. The bearers set the stretcher down beside the road, waiting for someone to collect him for interrogation if he didn't die first.

A cleanly dressed truck driver noticed that the wounded man had used what little strength he had left to struggle onto his side to take a piss. The driver waited for the trickle to start, then put the toe of his boot on the guy's shoulder to make him roll back and piss on himself. He laughed as the urine went all over the wounded man and seeped into his gut wound. Behind me, I heard the unmistakable sound of a rifle being racked. A Marine, possibly on the edge of reason from his last hill, aimed his weapon at the sadistic driver.

"No!" I shouted. I shared the rifleman's disgust, but I couldn't let him throw his life away by committing murder.

He lowered his weapon, spat on the ground, and walked back toward his buddies, who were getting ready for another hill.

It shames me that I did nothing but watch that happen. All I can do today is write about the cruelty this man suffered at the hands of a sworn defender of liberty and share a memory that has tormented me for most of my adult life.

* * *

In late March, I was up for promotion. That meant I had orders to report to the rear for a fitness test. I was looking forward to my first shower in a month. But mostly, I wanted to know how my buddy Second Lieutenant Cary Cowart was doing. Leading from the front, Cary had run ahead of his mortar section to observe where their rounds were landing. He was spotted by an enemy patrol and was sprayed with bullets from a "burp" gun, a toy-sized submachine gun so named for spitting out bullets so fast they slur together in a burping sound. Considering how badly he was hit, I couldn't understand why our doctors would keep him in a tent hospital instead of sending him rearward to more sophisticated facilities. As soon as the jeep I was riding in reached headquarters, I asked about my buddy.

An orderly checked a list, and said, "Lieutenant Cowart died last night."

Cowart was dead, and I got to take a shower. I felt sick.

A large squad tent marked "officers" housed rows of showerheads pouring out cascades of hot water. I stood at the tent-flap entry for a moment, not quite believing there was this much water anywhere on earth. There was a trellised table loaded with towels and clean uniforms. I left my carbine, my pistol, my boots, and my dungarees at the entry. I paused and looked at the other clothes, discarded by men from the rear who were already showering. We might as well have been wearing different uniforms. Their skivvies were clean and looked comfortable, mine had brown stains in the back. Cary's must have been bloody.

I got under the hot shower. Another naked guy, an older, wizened little fellow, entered and began his shower. He must have noticed my grimy gear.

"It's quiet up there these days," he said.

I tensed up and muttered something like, "Is that right?" All I could think about was Cowart. I added, "It's nice to be back here in the rear with all the deep thinking big-picture geniuses."

Unperturbed, he gave me his forecast, "Gooks will be pouring down around us any night now."

About then, a man came in whom I recognized as Colonel Sealy, a Regiment biggie who had visited the battalion. I remembered his name as it was the same as my mother's maiden name. He nodded to the man I had just mouthed off to and said, "Hello, Sir."

Sir...that meant he was talking to a general. I realized the short guy was none other than General Lewis B. "Chesty" Puller, recipient of more real medals than a dozen other generals, a veteran of WWI, the "Banana Wars," and WWII, hero of Guadalcanal and the Chosin Reservoir.

I left that tent so fast I must have been lathered with soap while scrambling into my new gear. I grabbed my weapons and made myself scarce. After passing my physical, I returned to the battalion a First Lieutenant.

On the night of April 21, I sent a note to Mary, brimming with overconfidence:

My Darling—

Just a note to say that I'm o.k.—We moved quite a way today & continue on tomorrow—w/any luck we should be north of Hwachon (sic), North Korea tomorrow.

I'm exhausted & will hit the sack—I love you, my wife—take it easy.

—Your mick

But we would get no farther north. Chesty was right. Just before midnight on April 22, Chinese and North Korean troops poured over the entire UN line in well-organized human wave attacks. The offensive had been scheduled for late May, but it was launched early because Chinese generals feared an American amphibious landing to their rear. Their strategy—as recorded in Professor Xiaobing Li's *China's Battle for Korea: The 1951 Spring Offensive*—was to "divide, encircle, and annihilate." The Chinese used night attacks and scale to overwhelm. But the Chinese's overwhelming numbers were just part of their effectiveness. Not only could they surround us, but they could do so completely undetected. They moved at night, safe from our air support. By "they," I'm referring to hundreds of thousands of troops, a whole army. At Chosin they had successfully marched over a quarter million men and supporting artillery into position without anyone noticing. The human wave attacks of the 1951 spring offensive involved 305,000 Chinese and 35,000 North Koreans.[2]

The Chinese planned to win the war with this huge spring offensive, securing a decisive victory within seven days. Once committed to the assault, they had no choice but to win and win quickly. American air support would make adequate resupply virtually impossible for them. Each man in Mao's army carried just twenty rounds of ammunition for the offensive; the five armies of the Chinese Ninth Army Group ran out of food just five days into the assault.

When the offensive kicked off, the US Army's 2nd Division and South Korean forces on our flanks bugged out, leaving our regiment cut off and surrounded. Each Marine battalion set up interlocking bands of machine-gun fire to defend their position on all sides. We were surrounded but not annihilated. The massive Chinese breakthrough in April turned out to be their last great effort to win the war. From that point on, the war became a series of costly, unnamed, and indecisive battles, many of which had higher UN casualty rates than Chosin. Mao changed his strategy from annihilation to attrition. The Chinese spring offensive taught his army the same lesson it had so painfully taught our forces the previous autumn: the war could not be won quickly, if at all.

---

2   2 Xiaobing Li, *China's Battle for Korea: The 1951 Spring Offensive.*

Whether attacking or defending, the Chinese liked to get close to us so we would be unable to call for air support or artillery without hitting our own men, thus negating our biggest technological advantage. Sometimes our pilots would drop ordinance on friendlies by accident with terrifying and horrible results. To lessen the chance of this, the Marines would put one of our pilots on the ground with each Marine infantry battalion. We always called our guy "Ace." Pilots must have hated when it was their turn, but we liked to know that at least they had a personal stake in not firebombing Marines.

Pilots could strafe the hill with their wing-mounted machine guns and bless the men they hit with a quick death, but their most effective weapon was napalm, the infamous jellied gasoline—designed in a lab at Harvard University in 1942—that sticks to human skin and burns at up to 2,200 degrees Fahrenheit. "Nape" was cased in oblong canisters, under the wings of fighter-bombers, that tumbled through the air when released, end over end with no fins to guide them because they didn't need guidance. Two 150-gallon napalm bombs would roast every living thing in an area the size of a football field. Direct hits weren't necessary, because even those lightly touched by the evil concoction were out of business.

Napalm kills by burning as well as hyperthermia and asphyxiation as it sucks up all the breathable air around its flames. This makes it effective against caves and bunkers. Anyone who isn't barbecued dies from lack of oxygen. It flows downhill, into trenches and holes, so there's nowhere to take cover. I don't have the words to describe the screams and the stench. Napalm is stuck to my memory, and it is still burning after all these years. My dreams are disfigured by it.

We once went through some ground that had been held by the

North Koreans. Due in part to the prior use of napalm, we met no resistance. The dead were burned black. One Marine put an unsmoked cigarette in a charred mouth, with still-white teeth, of a corpse suspended in the agony of immolation. As the hardened platoon passed the body, we cracked jokes:

"You want a light, buddy?"

"Be careful with those cigarettes, they'll make you cough."

"That last puff must have been a ballbuster."

"Is that filtered or unfiltered?"

To my shame, I laughed too.

★ ★ ★

Following the enemy breakthrough of the spring offensive, the 5th Marines were ordered to make a night-long retreat along the north-south ridges not yet occupied by the enemy who had charged through the broken lines elsewhere and rushed southward along the roads and trails in the valleys, intending to cut us off and surround us. We were moving south in a consolidation of the entire UN line, joining the forces who had abandoned us. I suggested to our commanding officer, Colonel Hopkins, that rather than abandon our food and ammo supply, which was too heavy to carry, I'd get a team together and take a truckload south over an unsecured road between the ridges. He okayed the move. I asked if he wanted to go along on what promised to be a tense and lonely ride in total darkness. He assured me he had better things to do than wait around while we loaded.

"Oh, really?" I responded, further endearing myself to this dandy whom we called "Hoppy" or "Idiot Six." (Six referring to O-6, Colonel.) He was a Stanford man full of arrogance, know-it-all-ism, and braggadocio concerning his alleged prowess in athletics and with the ladies. I often saw him in the front of the chow line, ahead of his men and officers.

Five or six of us loaded the open truck. I sat beside the driver, my carbine's safety off. The other four rode atop the load. No lights, no talking. We tried to move as stealthily and quickly as possible in a two-and-a-half ton "six-by" on the narrow road. Each shift of gears was an earsplitting ordeal. I didn't know whether to remain in the sheltering darkness and risk driving into a ditch or switch on the lights and make a dash for it. I chose darkness. After we'd crept southward for an hour or more, the exhausted driver missed the invisible edge of the crude road. The right-side wheels churned. We lurched to the right and came to a stop in a small ditch. Now we were literally in the shit.

One Marine stood security with his Browning Automatic Rifle (BAR) while the rest of us strained to unload some of the ammo to lighten the truck. Somehow, after a couple of hours' work, we wrestled the vehicle back onto the road and continued our lonesome journey. Near dawn, we reached the new perimeter. We were lucky not to have been gunned down by friendly fire, as "Idiot Six" had neglected to tell the defenders we were en route. I later learned that "Hoppy" got a medal for our action.

With first light came cover from Navy and Marine Corps flyers in gorgeous gull-winged Corsairs. Knowing that we were now resupplied and supported by air, the enemy sought softer targets elsewhere.

During the lull that followed, I congratulated my team on our successful journey. I had a memorable chat with one of them, the irreverent PFC Olsen. "Hey, Lieutenant, I know how I got in the Marines: I was drunk out of my fucking mind. Why did you join?"

"Well, it was something about getting my American citizenship and a college degree from the G.I. Bill for sitting on my ass in the Navy during the war that made me think I should sign up and be ready to do something in case the country needs me."

"Lieutenant, if we get out of this alive, will you be pulling that flag out of your ass?"

"I plan to."

Around that time, General MacArthur is quoted as saying, "I have just returned from visiting the Marines at the front, and there is not a finer fighting organization in the world." It couldn't have been our battalion he was talking about. When he visited our CP, Corporal McCauley—who should have been a sergeant but had a habit of getting busted back down to corporal—pulled a stocking cap down over his face so he couldn't be identified and shouted down the hill where "Mack," in his gold-braided cap, was meeting with regimental officers, "Put me in, coach, I can run!"

McCauley was referring to the US Army's 2nd Division's April 22 bailout that earned them the name "MacArthur's track team."

Marines are nothing if not funny. Alternative names for USMC include "Useless Sons Made Comfortable" and "Uncle Sam's Misguided Children."

★ ★ ★

The war supplied no shortage of grim reality checks to one's patriotic pretensions. During the retreat, my friend Jim Ables was accidentally shot in the back by one of his own men who failed to put his weapon on safe. The trigger snagged on something while they climbed onto a tank for a ride. Jim fell off the tank onto the road. I ran over just in time to hear him gasp a final word, a cliché of war movies and novels that happens to be something dying men really say: "Shit."

★ ★ ★

Jim had loved his home state of Texas. Leading patrols, his first three checkpoints were Tango, Echo, X-ray, followed by Alpha, Sierra. I would later learn that Ables had worked for O.C. Fisher, a useless congressman from Texas's twenty-first district. A dozen years later, while I was working in Kennedy's West Wing, I paid a visit to Fisher's office. No sooner could I mention Ables than this blowhard sounded off in a loud drawl about how he knew Ables died gloriously keeping us safe from the communists. He assembled his entire staff in his office and prompted me to regale them about Ables's heroic end. By then I had lied to Gold Star mothers and wives about the circumstances of their beloveds' deaths—I had let them think it had been great or purposeful or that their boys hadn't suffered or gone out screaming.

"That's not what happened," I said. "Jim died because another Marine's safety was off, and it was fucking tragic and awful, and his last words were 'shit.'"

Looking back, I know I shouldn't have used those bitter words, but I loved Jim and didn't know how to handle the way this slob was talking about him.

Ables's death was infuriating and painful, but there was more bad news that morning. Apparently, Colonel "Hoppy" had panicked during a night attack on Bravo Company. He ordered a tank to fire on a hill that Marines had already taken, wounding several. He relived the incident, telling me how wonderfully he had performed under great personal pressure. All I could do was stare at him.

I would soon get some satisfaction when "Idiot Six," resplendent in pressed dungarees, organized a volleyball game between the line officers and the headquarters of Charlie Company. Pete McCloskey arranged for me to play with the line officers. My turn came to play at the net. All six feet two inches of the Colonel towered overhead to block my mighty spike. I missed the ball, and somehow my fist went through the net and got him right in the mouth, putting him on his back. Pete McCloskey noticed my bruised knuckles and quietly observed that he hadn't known spikes were delivered with a closed fist. He didn't know that I had hoped to break bones so the Colonel would be taken out of the fight for a while, thus saving the lives of Marines who might die due to his incompetence and self-serving leadership.

Near Wonju with Pete McCloskey (right). The bulges in our pockets are hand grenades.

The next day, I was transferred out of Charlie Company's supply to become the mortar section leader of Charlie Company, supporting the rifle platoons with 60mm rounds lobed with limited accuracy and effectiveness from portable mortar tubes.

The company had been on the defensive for several weeks. Then the rest of the UN Army got its act together and began to cut into the overextended Chinese and North Korean supply lines. We moved north in careful pursuit of the erstwhile victors.

In his history of the Korean War, the late David Halberstam describes the situation that spring, 1951:

> "The war had settled into an unbearable, unwinnable battle; it had reached the point where there were no more victories, only death."[3]

It may have seemed unbearable, but both sides bore it. War is all about bearing the unbearable. Often discomfort, whether from cold or rain or lack of hot food, is what breaks a man when heaped upon the many other stresses and fears of combat. One reason they stopped executing men who broke down on the line after WWI was that psychologists came to understand that given enough time "in the shit," the psychiatric casualty rate will reach 100 percent in any unit.[4]

In May, Charlie Company's current second platoon leader got surrounded on patrol and couldn't figure a way out. He had been an otherwise brave, competent lieutenant. What happened to him could've happened to any of us. Nevertheless, the lieutenant in question would carry, for decades, the guilt of what happened on that patrol. They say that in all forms of violence, from war down to domestic abuse, survivors feel guilty no matter what they

---

3   David Halberstam, *The Coldest Winter: America and the Korean War.*

4   Dave Grossman, *On Killing: The Psychological Cost of Learning to Kill in War and Society.*

do or fail to do. That's just how humans process these things. The lieutenant froze. So what? Does he give an order that gets his guys killed? Does he make a courageous stand against an overwhelming enemy force and get the whole platoon rubbed out? Does he retreat? To where? He is lost.

By radio, our company commander, "Spike" Schening, relieved the officer, telling him to hand over the platoon to his sergeant and wait for rescue. Spike was a careful man who always insisted on neatly packed knapsacks, clean dry shaves, and the burial of every ration can or cigarette butt. He never shouted, but a look from Spike was enough. A grimace from him was like a form of corporal punishment. His only nonregulation gear was a carved walking stick that underscored his "walk in the park" attitude toward danger. Spike was a "Mustang," a Marine who had started as a boot (a private) and worked, or rather fought, his way up to commission as an officer. A veteran of Tarawa and Iwo Jima, a badass if there ever was one.

He was fond of telling us young lieutenants, "You amateurs are screwing up my profession."

Spike had Pete McCloskey take one rifleman and find the lost platoon and guide it back to our position. When that was done, Spike sent a runner for the relieved officer to join him, along with his radio man, his executive office, and a couple of others on an exposed hilltop. Normally Spike was not reckless, but he had one unfortunate habit. He would not bend under actual or potential fire. There is a combat photographer's photo taken on that beautiful spring morning, showing Spike standing upright, leaning casually against the remains of a small tree that had been stunted by an earlier exchange of fire. He set an unfortunate example for those around to do likewise, breaking two of the most basic rules of movement in a war zone:

- Don't stand on a ridgeline.
- Don't silhouette yourself.

My mortar section was dug-in nearby. I got up from my hole to join the group on the ridge. Spike had just ordered the platoon leader who'd been relieved to take over my mortar section and gave me command of the platoon. Trying to make the change without hurting a good man or flattering me, Spike told us this switch was not a big deal, merely an exchange that would give each of us "civilians" a chance to learn yet another Marine job. As ordered, I left the group and headed toward second platoon's position in relative safety below the crest of the ridge. I had moved no more than fifteen or twenty yards when a single shell exploded on the ridgeline. An enemy spotter must have found an irresistible target.

Everyone on the ridge had been hit. Half of my predecessor's clothes had been blown off. He was riddled with shrapnel and destined to wake up in hospital to begin a long stay. Spike was still on his feet, but he had no helmet and a nasty head wound with lots of blood but no brains showing. Years later, Spike would get hit again, this time in Vietnam. At one of our Charlie Company reunions, I asked him what happened.

"The same fucking thing! I was standing on a hill out in the open and they blew me up."

Others were stunned but less seriously wounded.

When a Marine in charge goes down, the maps are passed on to the next in line. Spike looked at his executive officer and mumbled, "You know where the maps are."

Then he went down, dazed, and drifting in and out.

Our company got a new commander, Richard Wagner, and I got my rifle platoon.

ON POINT

MAY 1951

"Panic sweeps my men when they are facing the American Marines."
—CAPTURED NORTH KOREAN MAJOR

In the first days of May 1951, we made a cautious advance, rotating the lead company within the battalion, the lead platoon within the company, the lead squad within a platoon, the lead four-man fire team within a squad, and the lead man within a fire team. On a given day, it could be a lone rifleman's turn walking point ahead of all friendly forces in the country.

By that time, we had shed our winter parkas and crawled out of our arctic sleeping bags. The weather alternated between hot and dry and hot and wet. The hills were slick and taxing to climb, and the muck made them miserable to sleep on. The terrain and weather had been described by Marine General Thomas as "never designed for polite warfare." For all the humidity, drinking water was scarce and water discipline was enforced.

Boredom consumed us on days of patrols and probes with no contact. Men got exhausted from digging, and then the battalion would move a couple hundred yards and they'd have to dig another line of holes. I tried to keep the men focused and made sure the Corpsmen checked their feet. If we came to a creek, we could strip down and take turns washing while the rest provided security. In one such spot, we came upon a dead Korean face down in the water. A sergeant advised, "Don't worry, his ass is pointed upstream."

Night was a tender time. The enemy moved on the hills around us using bugles to communicate, relay messages, and drive the point home that we were often surrounded by them. The enemy were good at moving silently, sometimes able to enter a fighting hole undetected. One night they snatched a guy from Pete McCloskey's platoon, right out of his two-man hole. His partner awoke to find him gone, never to be heard from or accounted for. His name is absent from POW records, and there was no body. Something like that will keep you awake. For a while at least. I slept with my revolver, the leather holster modified so I could pull the trigger if necessary and fire through my sleeping bag without having to draw the weapon.

Normally, we kept 50 percent watches, meaning that one man slept while the other man in his hole kept watch. This works great as long as the man on watch stays awake. If he drifts off, it becomes a zero percent watch. It is the platoon leader or sergeant's job to keep this from happening. We would crawl from hole to hole in the dark checking on the men, a great way to get your head blown off by a nervous and sleep-deprived Marine.

At night, no one made a sound above a whisper. No one except PFC Olsen, now in my rifle platoon. Darkness and silence gave him time to reflect on his impulsive and drunken enlistment, and he would yell into the void, "Four fucking years! I must have been nuts. Four fucking years!"

Not long after the war, I was walking on Market Street in San Francisco and heard, "Four fucking years!" shouted from across the street. "Just wanted to say hello, Lieutenant," Olsen called out as he kept walking.

Other than the dark, I had one great fear: land mines. More specifically, I feared one particular wound they tend to inflict. There's an antipersonnel mine known as the "bouncing betty," which shoots a light charge up from the ground to around waist height before detonating. It's designed to wound and maim, not to kill. From a tactical point of view, it's as brilliant as it is evil, because a wounded man takes his whole fire team out of action as they work to stabilize and move him.

Walking through my first minefield, I kept one hand deep in my pocket, subtly clutching my "brains." Sometimes when a guy loses his hand in combat, it's because he was using it to cover something even more valuable to him.

The Marines, in typical fashion, laugh in the face of "The Wound" with a crude marching cadence:

"There's always a Marine who will answer the call

Of a woman whose husband has no balls at all.

No balls at all!

No balls at all!

A very short penis and no balls at all."

★ ★ ★

In mid-May, the enemy began a series of offensives—or counter-offensives, or counters to our counteroffensives, it was getting hard to keep track—and each battalion of the 5th Marines put a screening company out in front of the line to head off nightly enemy assaults. Our regiment dug in on a series of hilltop circles. Machine gunners set up interlocking bands of grazing or plunging fire, alert to blast away all night. According to the rear echelon geniuses, we were still facing no less than 125,000 enemy.

Sometimes the enemy flowed around us, chasing bits and pieces of retreating US and South Korean Army units. When they did attack our positions directly, they suffered tremendous losses. In the morning after an assault, there were piles of bodies in front of our lines.

★ ★ ★

On the night of May 16, we faced one of the most intense enemy attacks yet. Again, we were left isolated by poorly trained, poorly led allies fleeing on our flanks. Shortly before dusk, when we would lose our air cover, I radioed a Corsair fighter/bomber pilot circling overhead.

"See many gooks?" I asked him.

"I see a shitload more gooks than Marines."

We set up positions in a circle prepared to fight in all directions. As friendly units failed to hold the line against these attacks, it became our mission to clean up after them, and to protect the now exposed flank where the Army or UN forces had been. The gulf in talent between the Marine Corps and the Army was astounding. After one assault where the enemy flowed around us and wiped out elements of the 8th Army, our patrol came to a field of slaughtered soldiers, in and around ravaged tents. Tents! What were they doing pitching tents in such an exposed position? A few dazed survivors milled about. A sergeant from our company spoke to an Army officer.

"What the fuck happened here?"

"It was every man for himself."

"Every man for himself? Jesus H. Christ!"

★ ★ ★

What the Army lacked in leadership, they more than made up for in nice new equipment. It's a point of pride that we Marines do our thing on a tight budget. We cost Uncle Sam less per man than any branch of the armed forces, and at the same time have higher standards for fitness and marksmanship.

One day, in the rear, I borrowed a jeep and trailer with Corporal McAuley and went on a treasure hunt. We found an Army supply dump including ammunition belts, grenade pouches (we had been using our pockets). A grunt's Christmas! As we loaded everything we could into the jeep, we were caught in the act by an Army POG.

"What do you men think you're doing?"

"Don't fuck with me," I said. We kept on scrounging, ignoring him.

When we returned to the battalion, a chaplain was conducting a hillside memorial service for Ables. We honored Jim with this gift of stolen goods, which we presented to his men after the service like some holy offering.

Once, when we came across some dead Army, I suggested removing their boots, which were far better than ours. We had been issued horrible boots with rubber seams that would cause blisters. Our feet froze in the cold and rotted with sweat in the heat. The Army, on the other hand, had relatively comfortable and weather-appropriate footwear. In the harsh and simple calculus of war, our squeamishness and shame about peeling boots off dead men was less than our discomfort walking in rotten ones.

More than sixty years later, I was to pay for this petty theft, in retirement, at a community center, on Cape Cod, playing pickle ball. I had forgotten my tennis shoes, thinking they were in my gym bag. A friend who was about my size had an extra pair.

I was lacing them up on the sidelines when a lump gathered in my throat, my pulse quickened, and I began to breathe hard.

"Fuck this," I muttered and excused myself to the parking lot where I broke down, overcome by the memory of the last time I put on another man's shoes.

★ ★ ★

Toward the end of May, following their failed Spring Offensive, the Chinese and North Koreans changed tactics. They dug into defensive positions on hilltops and waited for us to do the attacking. They got fresh troops and supplies, planted mines, obstructed trails, and made poor man's barbed wire with piles of brush and branches that they often booby trapped by tying branches to the pins of grenades that would detonate when we tried to clear the path. Jack Jones, the best ever battalion executive officer, who had been a Marine since he was a teenager, received the last of his five Purple Hearts, in his second war, for losing a piece of his hand to such a trap while trying to help a radioman clear a path.

★ ★ ★

Around May 15, we received replacements. Newcomers usually didn't last long, and their losses were less painful if we didn't get to know them.

Before going out on one patrol, I noticed that one of the greenest replacements was so nervous that he was shaking. Against standard operating procedure and the obvious wishes of my platoon sergeant and squad leaders, I ordered that the kid, who looked about twelve, was to stay behind to guard the packs. On a short patrol you leave behind your heavy pack, which contains living essentials, such as a sleeping bag and rations, and walk with a weapon, a belt carrying grenades, ammo, a first aid kit, and water. Normally, a sore-footed platoon rotates the easy and safe duty of watching the packs, with priority given to anyone who's due to head to the rear soon or who gives signs of urgently needing a break. My order to leave the kid behind was unfair to the guys who had made it this far without any serious scrapes and could have doomed one of them to have his luck run out.

Fortunately, the patrol was without incident. However, when we returned from our walk, the new kid was gone. McCloskey came over to tell me what happened. After we left, the kid had gone over to Pete's platoon to shoot the shit with a fellow replacement. The kid sat on a land mine.

We sent the dead lad's pack to the rear, where sensitive articles such as condoms would be removed before whatever personal items it may have contained were sent to his next of kin. He was so new that not one of us could recall his name. Pete and his platoon sergeant thanked me. The boy had cleared a mine for us without even nicking anyone else.

Later that month, when a fresh batch of replacements hiked past our position on their way to the company command post, I turned my back to avoid even looking at them, but one in particular noticed my averted eyes.

"It's a fine thing to travel thousands of miles to find someone and he won't even say hello."

Douglas Dacy, a buddy from PLC, stepped out of their ranks. I recognized his Texas drawl. Dacy was already a veteran of WWII, the son of a Lebanese immigrant who had sent all his boys to war by way of thanking America for its generosity. Dacy was also the heir to a small fortune and had used his privilege to get into the fighting rather than avoid it. His place in the infantry was secured, as a favor to his father, by then Senator Lyndon Baines Johnson. During his first week in Korea, Dacy was lightly wounded by shrapnel. He didn't report that wound because he was afraid he'd get a Purple Heart, then if he got another after that he might be sent home.

When Dacy deployed, he visited Mary to tell her, "I'm going to look after Chuck."

A runner followed Dacy and the replacements up the hill with a telegram for me:

PLEASE PASS TO LT CHARLES U. DALY 050418 X SON MICHAEL

WEIGHING 5 POUNDS 12 AND 3/4 OUNCES BORN SATURDAY 19 MAY AT 2:06 PM X A BLACK-HAIRED MICK X MARY AND MICHAEL BOTH FINE X LOVE MARY

Pete had received news about a baby daughter two days before. Our platoons were delighted. They said "we" made a baby. It was good news and it was tough news. I folded up the telegram and put it in my wallet and thought it'd be nice to have if I made it.

Now that note belongs to Michael's first daughter, my first grandchild, Sinéad.

A MEDAL AND A CRIME

MAY 29–JUNE 2, 1951

"I have long ago given up telling people what I saw them (the Marines in Korea) do on so many occasions. Nobody believes me, nor would I believe anyone else telling the same story of other troops."

—MAJOR GENERAL W.S. BROWN, USMC

Every year on my birthday, May 29, Pete McCloskey gives me a call to tell me, "You should have died today." Sometimes he adds, "You miserable son of a bitch." I dredge up some old comeback, and we reminisce about what happened on that day in 1951. My citation puts it like this:

> The President of the United States of America takes pleasure in presenting the Silver Star to First Lieutenant Charles U. Daly (MCSN: 0-50418), United States Marine Corps, for conspicuous gallantry and intrepidity as Leader of a Rifle Platoon of Company C, First Battalion, Fifth Marines, FIRST Marine Division, in action against enemy aggressor forces in Korea on 29 May 1951. Assigned the mission of driving a strong enemy force from well-entrenched positions on a high knob north of Inje, First Lieutenant Daly boldly led his men up a narrow spine, completely devoid of cover and concealment, and carried out a successful assault against the hostile strong points in the face of fierce automatic-weapons and small-arms fire, killing

many of the enemy and forcing the remainder to retreat in disorder. Quickly reorganizing his unit, he pursued the fleeing hostile troops and overran an enemy regimental command post, capturing many valuable documents and prisoners. By his marked courage, skilled leadership and unswerving devotion to duty, First Lieutenant Daly served to inspire all who observed him and upheld the highest traditions of the United States Naval Service.

Those words omit the parts of that day I would go on reliving, the guilt over what I did and what I didn't do, and the feeling that the bravest thing I did, that any of us did, was just keep moving uphill into gunfire. My citation leaves out a war crime I committed, a crime for which I was only punished with haunting memories. There's no mention of the men on both sides who died or sustained awful wounds for my red-white-and-blue ribbon with a star dangling from it. The citation praises me for "killing many enemy," but it leaves out just how hard it is to get young men to fire accurately, or at all, so that they kill other young men. It's unnatural to stand up "in the middle of flying metal," as Navy Cross recipient, Karl Marlantes, relates in *What It Is Like to Go to War,* but it's also unnatural to hurl metal at a boy who's scared like you, or to stick him with a metal blade 'til he dies, or to lob grenades—designed to be roughly the size of a baseball for familiarity's sake—and flay him with shards of metal. The "rules" of war are unnatural. They tell you *not* to kill a man who has surrendered, even when he's gravely wounded and probably going to die anyway and his pitiful screams tell you that killing him would be an act of mercy. The Department of the Navy makes no mention of my after-action duties, which included going through the pockets of enemy dead looking for intelligence and in one case finding a picture of a man's wife and his baby.

May 29 was a beautiful morning after a chilly and tense night. I turned twenty-four, possibly my last birthday. It was my platoon's turn to lead the company into what we had been told was an area held by an enemy regiment. Our objective was to take an exceptionally rugged hill. There was a cliff just west of the top and a steep, exposed slope to the east. Our only way up was a narrow spine with all cover and concealment long since blasted away. General Thomas concluded that enemy resistance in the hills, such as this one, around what was called the Kansas Line would be "broken not by air power but by Marine riflemen."[5]

Roger that!

At first light, I can remember thinking that we were facing a great defensive position. I had company when I stepped off the trail to take a piss after we dropped packs and were getting ready to move out and up. The air was tense. Even the chattiest Marines were silent. The smokers puffed up a storm. I wondered if the North Koreans could smell Lucky Strikes on our men as we could sometimes smell garlic on theirs.

With two words you don't hear very often in modern combat, I gave the order: "Fix bayonets."

That didn't help anyone's peace of mind. But I liked bayonets for the scare factor. I knew that frightening the enemy was a good way to keep young men from getting killed on both sides.

Warner, the new company commander, who was even greener than me, offered to call in an air strike if we got into trouble. I declined, pointing out that strikes had been recently put under

---

5   *US Marine Operations in Korea*, Vol. IV.

Army command and were running late, with the habit of hastily dumping their loads on friends and foe alike. Any delay in air or artillery would leave us exposed under fire. The only course of action was to get in among the enemy so *their* support—mortars, guns, and heavy weapons—would have to be lifted.

My job was to keep the men moving up and firing. I talked with my platoon sergeant whose advice was essential, because if a major firefight took place, it would be my first. We agreed that if we came under fire, the lead squad would charge directly up the spine, second squad would fire everything they had at the ridge to the west of the hill, and third squad would continue the charge led by first squad. The machine gun section attached to the platoon would follow and set up on the hilltop as soon as it was secure to fend off any counterattack. We had received several reports that elsewhere, a North Korean had played dead and shot a couple of Marines in the back after they walked past. I wanted to make sure that didn't happen to any of us, so I passed the word: "If they don't stink, stick 'em."

At 08:00 we began slowly climbing up the ridge, single file on the narrow trail. There were small pines and some saplings blown leafless by earlier shelling. To delay our advance, branches were piled on the path, forming poor man's barbed wire. No birds sang. I was walking close behind the first squad when we came to a small knoll at the base of the much larger hill that loomed above. Billy Bell, an experienced rifleman from Arizona, got ready to toss a grenade over the crest of the knoll just in case there was an ambush waiting there. Not wanting to alert the enemy to our advance and afraid of seeming trigger-happy in a situation where there might be no enemy, I knocked my wedding ring against the stock of my carbine to get Bell's attention and hand signaled "No grenade." He put the grenade back in his pocket and resumed quietly leading our first fire team over the crest of the hill in a crouched walk.

In an instant, Bell went down under a shower of enemy grenades and bullets. The rest of the fire team rolled off the rise, and those of us who weren't shocked into inaction began shooting.

"Fire. Fire. Shoot, Goddamnit! Fire!"

"Bell is down."

"Grenade."

"Shit. I'm hit."

"Corpsman! Help."

"Keep going. Fire. Fire. Fire. Kill those cocksuckers!"

"They're bailing out."

"I'm out of ammo!"

"Use your fucking bayonet. Keep going. Stick 'em. Fire, Goddamnit, fire!"

I figured the louder we were, the more we'd give the impression that we were a huge force determined to kill anyone standing between us and the Yalu River. The sound of two dozen or so riflemen firing all at once is impressive.

Dacy would later recall, "It sounded like World War Two up there."

I let loose all the rounds in my carbine, aiming uphill at no particular target. I reversed my magazine and loaded a second that I had taped to it for faster reloading and resumed firing at nothing, adding to the din. An unlucky North Korean popped up in front of me from a hole. His throat and jaw blew apart with the squeeze of my trigger finger.

A shout from my radioman, "The captain wants you. He's telling us to drop back and wait for artillery."

"Tell him to go fuck himself."

There were so many grenades being tossed down the hill at us that I thought we were under mortar fire. To stop would have been suicidal.

We reached the top. There were many enemy dead, wounded, and surrendering. I was wild with frustration because my caution on the knoll had been costly. With a few riflemen, I kept running over the far side of the hill in pursuit of some fleeing enemy. We were astounded to find our charge had put us among a bunch of enemy officers with maps still in their hands as though they had been in a routine review of their position. Unbelievable. Another unarmed enemy officer crawled out of a command bunker and started berating his comrades, apparently upset that they were surrendering to this handful of exhausted Marines. One version of what happened next appears in a chapter about me in McCloskey's *The Taking of Hill 610*:

> "Daly personally pushed the captured and surly Korean commander off a 1,000-foot cliff."

That's the legend, and a prime example of how the truth gets warped by memory and the intense emotions of combat and its aftermath. Here's the facts as I recall them. I knew we had to shut this guy up before he got his men to realize that we were overextended, low on ammo, outnumbered, and extremely vulnerable. I figured he'd be less noisy with his clothes off, so I threatened the officer with my bayonet and motioned for him and his men to strip, which some of them proceeded to do. I have a picture of three of them, hands upraised, two clad in undershorts and one in longer underwear held together by a string that came undone revealing his limp dick. They look dazed and frightened. All the prisoners except the loud officer were tense but silent. Without warning, their leader turned, dashed over the cliff's edge, and may have been shot in the back by an alert rifleman. In any case, the major could run but he could not fly.

All firing had stopped. Except for picking up the pieces, this little battle was over. The pieces included Billy Bell's right arm. He sat leaning against a tree stump, calm and pale. A corpsman held a compress to his wound.

"I hope you're left-handed," I said, not knowing how else to express my concern without upsetting him.

"I am now, Lieutenant."

There were screams coming from a badly wounded North Korean laying close by. His dying was getting louder and louder, and I could sense how much the sound was upsetting my men.

A young corporal brought up the decent thing to do. "Lieutenant, do you want me to do him a favor?"

"Do it."

A shot. Then silence.

I knew then, and I know now, that shooting a prisoner, or ordering such a killing, is a war crime regardless of the victim's condition. I know that I should not have ordered it. I know that if it had to be done, I should have done it with my own weapon and protected my fellow Marine from having one more life on his conscience. I can still hear that shot.

After the murder came the next grim task, searching the pockets of enemy corpses for papers to send back to intelligence officers.

One enemy had half of his head missing. Dacy had come up and asked how I was doing. I grunted and pointed to the corpse.

In one pocket I found a picture of what must have been the man's wife and baby.

"Hey, Lieutenant, don't feel so bad," said David Ivens, a seasoned machine gunner who could see I was upset. "At least he got to see a picture of his baby."

I wondered if I would be so lucky.

I pocketed the three striped shoulder board of an officer I killed in the first moments of the battle. Dacy picked up an unexploded hand grenade that must have been thrown by a North Korean too frantic to pull the pin. Dacy disarmed it using a can opener, and when we met again back in the States, he gave it to me. I have used it as a paperweight ever since.

The chiggy bearers arrived with ammunition, water, rations, and our packs from the bottom of the hill. We sat and hydrated among the dead and wounded. Those who could eat, ate cold tinned rations for lunch. Everyone's favorite was the canned fruit cocktail. Some men would eat the fruit cocktail first in case they got wounded or otherwise had their meal interrupted. They would have at least enjoyed the best course.

I wrote a page or two about the day to my dad.

We had been followed by a combat cameraman who had been taking snaps all day and doing his best not to get hit.

"That was some day," he said. "If we get out of here, you might want to have the pack numbers for those photographs." I kept the numbers and later was able to obtain the prints.

Taking prisoners, May 29, 1951.

Elsewhere on the 29th, we lost lieutenants Munday and Buckmann, who on more than one occasion aboard the troop ship had said, "I'm going to die in Korea."

PFC Whitt L. Moreland, in McCloskey's platoon, was also killed on the 29th. He smothered a hand grenade blast with his body, saving the lives of the men around him, including Pete's. He was posthumously awarded the Congressional Medal of Honor.

★ ★ ★

There was another hill, a couple of days later, that we took with no resistance. Ivens was cleaning his machine gun a couple of feet above where I was sitting. We laughed about how easy this hill had been compared to May 29th. Easy, except a faulty radio left me out of touch with the rest of Charlie Company. McCloskey had sensed my problem and dispatched his own radioman, Rocky Bruder, up the hill to reestablish coms. Rocky paused to catch his breath just short of my position, winded and sweaty from his radio-laden climb.

"Get up here," I said.

Rocky grunted, moved the last few feet, and started to hand me the mic connected by a short wire to the radio on his back.

Somewhere from behind, a burst of machine gun fire smacked into us. First one blast, then the distant gunner adjusted his aim, *over one click then up one*, before firing the second burst. The first volley, to my right, hit Rocky in the back. The next, high and to my left, made Ivens's head explode.

Rocky mumbled, "Corpsman," in his last instant of life.

I could hear the call, "Gunner down, second gunner up," keeping the whole game moving smoothly but with two less players.

I believed then and I believe now that the lethal fire had come from our own distant machine gun. I should have known that might happen. I had been so anxious to establish radio contact because of how quickly we had taken the objective. I didn't want our gunners to mistake our movement near the crest of the hill for enemy defenders, not realizing there weren't any defenders.

Brain matter and blood were splattered all over me. In the coming days, every time I encountered water, in streams and rain, I would try to wash the stains off, but traces would remain until I was wounded ten days later and my clothes were cut away.

When Pete came up the hill and saw me splattered with blood and brains, he tried to calm me down.

"Beautiful day, isn't it?" he said.

War changes the meaning of normal in ways big and small. There's a joke about a Marine who comes home to his parents and says, "Pass the fucking butter" at the dinner table.

One June day, having rotated off the line, we watched an American tank approach a shallow river. We could sense the driver trying to decide whether to take a muddy bypass or stay on the road; either could have been mined.

We speculated out loud and made mock bets.

The tank took the detour. KABOOM.

A man flew out of the open hatch, now legless.

One of our riflemen shouted, "I win!"

★ ★ ★

On June 2, it was Pete's turn to take a hill. That task promised to be a shitshow from the first. The evening before the attack, Pete and I had watched the North Koreans register mortar shells on the narrow approach to the hill, meaning they had figured out exactly where to drop the shells so they could lob them continuously on anyone moving up.

Ordinarily a platoon takes care of its own wounded, but if Pete's guys slowed down to do that, they'd be slaughtered. They would have to keep moving no matter what, so Pete and I agreed that my platoon would get the wounded out of the shit. A breach of standard procedure, but the only sane thing to do in an impossible situation.

Shortly before the assault was to begin, Pete and I spoke on the comm wire, an open telephone line between the platoons. What could have been some of his final words shook me: "You know, I think this is gonna be my last hill."

"Don't say that, you're the best one left."

At which point Spike's replacement, our new captain, chimed in, "Hey, what does that mean?"

"Get off the line, Sir."

Again, I continued to urge Pete to keep moving no matter what, even if the captain or even our illustrious Colonel "Hoppy" ordered him to hold under mortar fire while he called in close air support.

That is precisely what happened.

I listened on the radio as Pete led the charge. Almost immediately, one Marine was hit. At the same time, I was ordered to retrieve a wounded Korean prisoner at Pete's position in hope of getting some intelligence from him. In situations like these, I had an unfair habit of relying on Gunther Dohse for the toughest tasks. Gunther was a German immigrant who had survived WWII and enlisted in the Marines, thinking he was joining the Navy. By the time I took over second platoon, Corporal "Gunner" Dohse was already a decorated combat veteran. I ordered him to send a fire team to check out Pete's wounded Marine and retrieve the prisoner. Not knowing that I had told Pete to keep his men moving forward no matter what, Dohse replied that he couldn't send his men into a situation that should have been handled by Pete's platoon.

"Marines 'do or die,'" he recalls, "but I had a mind of my own."

Here was Dohse, the best of Marines, disobeying his superior officer's direct order. I got frustrated and told him, "Get going, I'll go with you."

Under fire, alternately running and flopping down in the muck, we made our way across the rice paddy. The first words the wounded Marine, Private First Class Bob Aylmer, and I ever exchanged seemed likely to be our last.

"Hang in there," I said.

"I'm okay."

Okay? Aylmer had one eye dribbling out of its socket. His face was badly cut up, his knee blasted at a gruesome angle, torso torn. But through the blood and damaged jaw, he said it again.

"I'm okay."

What a mess. We now had to bring back two men under fire, and neither of them could walk. Dohse put the prisoner on his back in a fireman's carry and headed back. I grabbed Dohse's rifle and we splashed across the paddy, dropping several times when we received plunging rifle fire from the hill above. After we got to our side, Dohse took the prisoner to company headquarters. I sent a stretcher team, led by PFC Arthur Bennett, to retrieve Aylmer.

The next time I saw Bob Aylmer, I was on a stretcher too.

GOOD NEWS, CHUCK WOUNDED

JUNE 12, 1951

"What makes the green grass grow?"
"Blood! Blood! Blood!"

—MARINE CORPS CHANT

My brief career as a platoon leader ended early on the morning of June 12, 1951. I had spent the night of the eleventh—my second wedding anniversary—with my platoon manning a lonely outpost, ahead of our lines, just north of the town of Inje.

The platoon sergeant and I laid-up in an abandoned enemy bunker. Idiot Six had sent the battalion up a valley before the ridges above it were secure. An attack on our position that night could have doomed us, but it didn't come. I felt good. Even though I still had little hope of living to hold my son, a picture Mary had sent me of him had arrived in a letter enclosed with a melted Heath bar. Having seen my son Michael's face, I suddenly had more to lose. Dying was going to be hard.

At first light I told Sergeant Murphy that I was going out of the bunker to check our perimeter. He said he'd already done so a couple hours before. But I was restless and anxious about the strain of a 50 percent watch with no sergeants; all but Murphy had been killed, wounded, or rotated. I would tell the guys they could get some rest. I was getting up from my hands and knees after crawling out of the bunker when I sensed that I had company. I got up just as a bullet ripped across the front of my jacket and whacked into my left arm.

"Corpsman! The lieutenant's down."

I grabbed my arm above the wound and waited for the corpsman. There was no sign of a real attack. An unseen sniper had spotted an easy target.

The corpsman cut away my sleeve and revealed bones sticking through a red and pink mess. The arm was dangling below the elbow. I told him to cut it off.

"Not me," he said, tightening down the tourniquet.

I got on the radio to tell the company HQ what had happened. It was then that I learned the whole morning was a mess. Third platoon's leader had been hit with shrapnel from a mortar round. The battalion's new executive officer, Jack Jones, the real leader who kept the colonel somewhat in check, had a chunk of his right hand blown off by a booby trap hidden in poor man's barbed wire. Pete had been hit in the leg while helping one of his wounded. So, Charlie Company had no platoon leaders and the battalion had an unfettered idiot in command.

By now I was getting sore because the numbing impact of the bullet and the subsequent surge of adrenaline had worn off. Because of our isolated position, I decided to make my own way back to our lines rather than deprive our platoon of rifle-men carrying me off. I couldn't make that hike if I was stoned on morphine, so there would be no pain relief until I reached our lines. I started the walk to Battalion HQ, where I would be flown to a field hospital.

In Korea, helicopters were just coming into use and were too tiny and fragile to risk ahead of the lines to pick up those who got hit on outpost or on patrol. In every war since, improvements in helicopter capabilities have translated to saved lives and limbs. Now they can land much closer to the action and deliver wounded to advanced medical care within minutes.

On my way to the little bird, I had to walk through a shallow creek. I wasn't feeling great, but I felt worse when two rounds from a distant rifle struck the water near me. I turned toward the ridge where the shots had come from and gave the finger with my good arm. I don't know what, if anything, that sign means in Korea, but the shooting stopped.

At the command post, I saw a stretcher with McCloskey on it. He was all set to go farther to the rear, have his minor wound treated, get laid, and return to duty. He took one look at me, rolled off the stretcher, stood up, said a quick goodbye, and limped back up the valley to take over one or more of the remaining platoons. His own wound could wait.

I sat down and got my first morphine shot of the day. There was another Marine, I believe a platoon leader, on a stretcher. I asked him where he'd been hit.

"They got the family jewels."

While we waited for a chopper, I had visitors. A couple of my old chiggy bearers came to see me. One of them seemed very emotional.

Sergeant C.C. Vickers of headquarters company came to claim my pistol. On the day I met him, Vickers had admired my sidearm, saying, "Lieutenant, when you go down, can I have that pistol?"

I had replied, "I'll be carrying it while we're shoveling dirt on your face."

I could hear the chopper coming. I took the revolver off my belt and handed it to Vickers. In late 1952, while I was still in Navy hospitals recovering, Vickers found me. He walked in, set the pistol down on my hospital bed's nightstand, and walked away without saying a word.

A tiny helicopter whirled in, the kind with a bubble canopy you may know from the opening credits of the TV show *M*A*S*H*, the Bell 47. These choppers had two landing skids, each of which was fitted with an open wire basket, with room for one badly wounded or dead Marine. Inside the bubble sat the pilot beside a passenger seat for a wounded Marine who had to be conscious so as not to flop around and disturb the controls. The pilot motioned for me to sit beside him in the bubble, *thank God*. As I was being helped into the passenger seat, I noticed a bumper sticker on the cockpit's windshield:

Join the Marines!

We took off in a cloud of dust, which must have been tough on the men in the baskets. Within about ten or fifteen minutes, we set down near one end of a big brown tent. This was a Battalion

Aid Station, a field hospital staffed with Navy doctors, the Corps' answer to an Army MASH. Unlike *M*A*S*H*, the TV show, which fictionalized this aspect of the Korean war, there was no laughter in this tent, no cute nurses, no fun, just young men suffering in silence, each waiting for his stretcher to be lifted up and placed upon a pair of wooden saw horses of the sort used by carpenters to bring wood up to a convenient height for cutting. Each bloody stretcher became its own operating table. Between each set of stretchers stood dungaree-clad surgeons, working under gas lamps dangling from the tent ceiling beside bottles of blood plasma and IV fluid.

General anesthesia was rarely used. Speed was vital. The mission was to stabilize the patients who had the best chances for more advanced treatment elsewhere and comfort the ones who weren't going to make it. Aid Station doctors referred to their duty as "meatball surgery." At some of the stations, a corpsman or nurse would work on a foot or leg while the surgeon tended to a chest or head wound on the same man. I didn't notice much in the way of surgical gloves or hand washing between jobs. I noticed no stench, perhaps because I stunk.

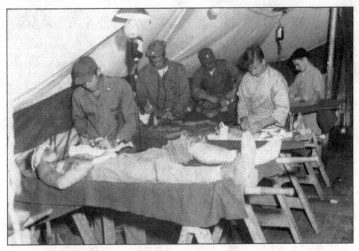

Navy docs and corpsmen perform "meatball surgery" in a Battalion Aid Station.

Outside the tent, as I waited to be seen, I heard the Marine next to me die. He didn't groan, just gasped, and stopped breathing.

The worst sound I heard that day was the clang of shrapnel being dropped onto the stainless-steel table beside the unlucky lieutenant's stretcher. The shrapnel had been removed from his groin.

"Keep that for me, Doc. I'll give it to my wife, and we'll push it around in a baby carriage."

The dead Marine was still uncovered when two corpsmen carried my stretcher inside and placed it on the sawhorses.

"How're you doin'?" a surgeon asked. He loosened the field dressing, resulting in a gush of blood.

"Doc, I can't go home lopsided. You're not going to cut it off, are you?" By now I was hoping to keep the arm.

"Not right now. We can wait for it to fall off."

Then he surprised me by gently touching my face with his bloody finger. That touch made my eyes water, so I turned my head. Tears return to my eyes today remembering that touch, a moment of tenderness amid all the suffering.

Outside the tent, waiting to be transported again, I had to piss, but I found I couldn't get up from the stretcher. I rolled on my side and did my best to aim for the dirt, not that pissing my pants could have made me smell any worse. I was marked as "patient baggage" with a baggage tag listing my rank, serial number, and destination hospital, and was loaded onto a stretcher rack inside a DC-3 cargo plane. I remember little about the noisy flight. I recall being on a train at some point, and I remember lying on a platform being winched up through the air by a crane and onto a ship.

I woke aboard the USS Haven in the late afternoon of what had been a very long day. On the table in a floating operating room, as clean and sophisticated as any hospital, I told a new doctor that I didn't want to go home to my wife and new baby missing an arm. It could be that he was postponing the inevitable, but without comment, he continued patching rather than amputate and scheduled me for transfer to a hospital in Japan.

That same night on the ship, after being washed, I was wheeled into a cabin where I rested in a bed, between white sheets, for the first time since February. I had been bleeding continuously all day, so I felt weak.

Like a figment of my morphine injections, Jack Jones appeared in my cabin. The doctors had just finished clipping away shredded bits of his hand, the final wound of five he had received since he enlisted at age seventeen in the last war. Jack had already scouted out the interior of the ship and knew where we could catch a movie in the officers' wardroom. We watched Indians chasing a battered group of cowboys on screen.

"That looks like the Chinese running us out of the North," Jack said.

Even without popcorn, it was a great way to end my longest day.

The next morning, June 13, we were flown to a former Japanese military hospital, in Yokosuka, Japan, for further patching up. We took a short walk outside the gate, where we found a little bar. Jack was a Mormon and didn't drink, but he watched me put a few back. The barman spoke English and told us he had fought on Iwo Jima.

"You were on Iwo," Jack said. "How come I didn't kill you?" Matter-of-fact without a hint of resentment or prejudice. The two of them sounded to me like high school athletes from rival towns catching up.

Meanwhile, at home, my father had been listed as my next of kin because I didn't want to shock Mary in the event I was KIA or wounded. That turned out to be a terrible idea. My mother went to Mary's apartment waving the telegram, "Good news, Chuck's been wounded."

Mum must have been thinking of her dead brother and brother-in-law, along with so many others in the meat grinder of Flanders and the Somme. In the Great War, survivable wounds were good news to families back in Blighty and Ireland. But my pacifist wife didn't see it that way. She was horrified, angry, and terribly worried.

From Japan, we were flown to Guam and then Hawaii. Before landing, the nurses had to confiscate our pants so we couldn't leave the hospital on base in search of fun. Jack knew this was part of the drill from experience, so he persuaded the young ladies to fold our trousers under the blankets on our stretchers.

With our smuggled pants on, we walked off the base for a big day and a long night in Hawaii. A kind nurse had helped me with the laces and buttons of my uniform. I got drunk easily since I was on morphine and was drinking for the second time in months. In a souvenir shop, I bought a bright Hawaiian shirt many sizes too big so it would fit over my sling. I would wear it as a gag getting off the plane to meet Mary, like I had been on vacation.

Back at the base, we were in deep shit with a red-faced Army officer, who gave us a lecture. "This base is no different from the front line. You are AWOL and there will be consequences. I will personally see to it that you are kept at this hospital until you rot."

The next day, a Marine general visited to pin Purple Hearts to our hospital gowns and deliver a few words about valor. "All of us admire your courage...You must be looking forward to getting home."

"Oh, no, sir," one of the group spoke up. "We've been promised to stay here 'til we rot."

"What?!"

He made sure we were out on the next flight. From Hawaii, we were flown to a hospital on Treasure Island, in San Francisco Bay, for several days. From there, to another hospital in San Antonio, where we underwent more repairs and celebrated the 4th of July in hospital beds. Distant fireworks were terrifying for a blinded Marine who awoke back in Korea but without his sight, his rifle, or his buddies.

Finally, we thumped down at Andrews Air Force Base, a few miles from the Naval Hospital in Bethesda and not far from my parents' home, loaded in stretchers stacked three high. My wound was still seeping, and my latest cast stank.

The plane's big side hatch opened to the bright sunshine. As I was helped to my turn at the top of the steep stairs, I could see a little crowd standing on the tarmac. There was Mary cradling a tiny bundle, Michael! Dressed in my Hawaiian shirt, I eased my way down the stairs, and gave her the best hug I could manage with my cast pressed against Michael in her arms.

We laughed. We cried.

I had orders to report for surgery, maybe even amputation. None of that mattered. I only needed one arm to hold my son.

My joy in that moment was tempered by the sight of my brothers being unloaded on stretchers, many without families to hold. One of those men on my flight was Bob Aylmer. After I kissed Mary and met my son, I waited for Bob's stretcher to be unloaded. I stayed by his side until he was in the care of Navy doctors.

Of my fellow Marines from the troop ship, Lieutenants Ables, Baumgart, Buchman, Cowart, Finch, Goudelock, McVeigh, Munday, Musser, Ohanessian, and Smith were killed in action. Many left wives with babies. Each widow got a $10,000 life insurance payoff plus a small pension. Not much, but a lot more than was received by the Chinese and North Korean widows we created.

Private First Class Henry Lee "Rocky" Bruder, from Illinois, now lies in Section 33 Site 11474 of Arlington National Cemetery.

David Darwin Ivens came from Canada and was already a veteran of World War II, having served in Canada's forces. He is buried in Beechmount Cemetery, Edmonton, Alberta.

Gunther "Gunner" Dohse eventually made sergeant and asked to have his tour in Korea extended. This extension was cancelled on November 27, 1951, when the Commandant of the Marine Corps ordered all Marines who had already spent one Christmas at war to return to the States. He became a mustang, leading his own platoon as a lieutenant in Vietnam. He also survived that souvenir hunt and retired as a captain. After that, he was an elementary school teacher, and then he became a master gardener and teacher of horticulture. He lives in the Pacific Northwest now, where he and his wife advocate organic food and sustainable, edible gardens. We email from time to time and have seen each other at reunions. In a recent message, he reflected on the enduring bond that came from just a few intense weeks of knowing each other. "The war threw us together for a couple of weeks, but we will carry our memories to the beyond."

Jack Jones and Billy Bell also became teachers.

After his wounding in Vietnam, Spike Schening joined the Red Cross, supervising disaster relief efforts in the sort of difficult places where he always felt at home. Beside the grenade on my desk, I have a silver-plated railroad spike to remember him by. The other "amateur" lieutenants under his tutelage all have one.

Years later, when Pete McCloskey returned to Korea for a peacetime visit, he climbed up the same hill he had taken in 1951. But he had to be carried back down; the hill was too steep, and his knees were too old.

A total of 4,267 Marines were killed in three years of fighting in Korea and 23,744 were wounded. The total number of Americans killed in action was 33,746, and 103,284 were wounded.[6] [7] Our South Korean allies lost 137,899.[8] The Chinese and North Koreans lost upwards of half a million. These numbers, though overwhelming, are dwarfed by the deaths of an estimated two to three million North and South Korean civilians.

Meditating on these numbers and the personal sacrifice behind each digit, I'm reminded of an epitaph John Maxwell Edmonds wrote for some men killed in my father's war:

"When you go home, tell them of us and say:

For your tomorrows, we gave our today."

---

6   In 1953, the Pentagon published the death toll as 54,260. This number accounts for 20,617 "other deaths" i.e., illness, accidents, etc., and military deaths worldwide while the Korean war was going on. The total number of Americans killed in action was 33,746. An additional 3,262 died in the warzone of noncombat-related-causes.

7   John W. Chambers II, ed., *The Oxford Companion to American Military History.*

8   Ministry of National Defense of Republic of Korea, "Casualties of Korean War" (in Korean).

PART II

BITTER SAFETY

BETHESDA

1951–1952

"When I'm asleep, dreaming and lulled and warm,
They come, the homeless ones, the noiseless dead.
While the dim charging breakers of the storm
Bellow and drone and rumble overhead,
Out of the gloom they gather about my bed.
They whisper to my heart; their thoughts are mine.
"Why are you here with all your watches ended?
From Ypres to Frise we sought you in the Line.
In bitter safety I awake, unfriended;
And while the dawn begins with slashing rain
I think of the Battalion in the mud.
"When are you going out to them again?
Are they not still your brothers through our blood?"

—"SICK LEAVE," SIEGFRIED SASSOON

People talk about the "Forgotten War" as if future generations of students and textbook authors didn't do their job. But the fact is few at home were thinking about Korea even when we were in it. The year 1951 was a year of wonderful distraction in America: *I Love Lucy* premiered and *The Catcher in the Rye* was published. There was a new Chevy on the market. There was no home front. The Greatest Generation, who had put their lives and comfort on hold to fight the last war, were buying suburban homes with G.I. loans and starting families in the most comfortable era in American history. Unemployment was 3.3 percent. There was no antiwar movement like there would be in the next war. Then, as now, few Americans could find Korea on the map. Today, most Americans don't know that there's never been an official armistice and that the Korean War is technically still going on as of this writing.

The complacency and indifference at home became clear to me on one of my first trips out of the Naval Medical Center in Bethesda, Maryland. I'd been given a pass to spend the night away. Mary and I stayed at the Tidewater Inn in beautiful Southern Virginia. In the bar at the Inn, some locals noticed my sling and cast and assumed I was the gentleman whose boating accident they'd read about in the local paper. I had to ask them to repeat the question. I suddenly didn't know where I was. I couldn't imagine pleasure boating mishaps any more than they could picture the circumstances of my wound. Before dinner, the house band played "Dixie" and everybody stood. I remained seated and breathed hard. Despite Mary holding my trembling right hand, I felt completely alone. I thought about Cowart and Ables, Rocky and Ivens, and longed to be with them, if not joining their ranks in death, at least back in the dirt cracking sick jokes and feeling like my work mattered. That feeling would return for a very long time. It's only recently, looking back with the perspective that comes from a lifetime of dwelling on the personal cost of "the game," as my slain Uncle Charlie called it, that I no longer wish to be back there with them but wish they could be here with me instead.

I was rated 40 percent disabled for my semi-useless arm according to a Veterans Administration chart that compensates one leg at one rate, two legs at another, and another for loss of sight or for one or both of "the brains" or a "three-piece set."

My therapy started when the seepage stopped. For a while, the closest thing I had to exercise was putting my arm in a warm whirlpool for hours. That wasn't pleasant, but not totally unpleasant. Eventually, my prognosis turned around and there were no more jokes about waiting for the arm to fall off. The Navy doctors were able to fuse the two bones in my forearm, the radius and ulna, into a one-bone forearm, resulting in an arm that can no longer pronate (twist). Progress was slow. Finger exercises were frustrating. For a while, I was motivated by the relief of knowing I could keep the limb. The reconstruction left my arm much more fragile than if I had both bones. With each fracture came the dread that I may be starting from square one with therapy. The bullet damaged the ulnar nerve, leaving me with a permanent "funny bone" feeling and an arm that's sensitive and somewhat painful when touched from the elbow down. Since then, I have worn my watch on my right wrist. Protecting the arm and holding it close and in front like it's in a sling has twisted my spine slightly over time. So today I use a walking stick when I feel I'm listing too far over. The official report describes it like this:

> "Malunion left forearm, incomplete paralysis of musculospiral nerve, limitation of flexion, limitation of extension hand, limited loss of pronation and supination."

While I was still in the hospital, my father insisted that I get the opinion of a civilian specialist to see if there was anything more that could be done. The specialist told me it was a miracle the Navy docs had been able to save my arm. I was grateful for that, but what bothered me at the time was that I couldn't hold Michael properly. On one of my early trips home, I was walking around our tiny apartment with him. I tripped trying to close a door with my foot. Rather than drop Michael, I fell on my arm. The docs set my broken arm, and the healing started over.

One brilliant thing military hospitals do is put every patient in contact and close quarters with fellow wounded, many of whom are maimed in ways that make you thankful for your own condition. As much as my hydrotherapy tickled, I could never compare my discomfort to the tortured grit of fellows with missing limbs trying to run, walk, or swim again. So what if I couldn't hold Michael properly? Some other Marines couldn't ever have kids. I saw one badly disfigured lieutenant hold a mirror to inspect the results of multiple plastic surgeries, the way you would in a barber's chair. With despair in his voice, he pleaded with the doctors, "This is all you can do for me?"

John C. Fryer, whom I met in therapy, had lost a leg along with most of his hands to a Chinese grenade.

He had asked the man who found him, a Mexican American private, to leave him and save himself. The Latino kid pulled a crucifix out from around his neck. "I will never leave you," he vowed.

Before the war, Fryer had been a fisherman in Alaska, ironically America's most dangerous job. When he returned from a long trip, a buddy met him on the dock and said, "Hey, John, let's go to war."

"What war?" Fryer asked.

While we were in Bethesda, I asked Fryer what he would do if that buddy had asked him to go back to war, knowing exactly what would happen. Without hesitation, he said he would go.

The first time Fryer was up and walking on his prosthetic leg, Mary and I had him over for dinner. When Mary saw him off his crutches she exclaimed, "John, you're so tall!"

He smiled and stood even taller.

Fryer had dreamed of being a forest ranger after the war. I've always hoped he made that happen with one leg.

The last thing I heard Bob Aylmer say, when Gunther Dohse and I rescued him from that rice paddy, was, "I'm okay." Bob was okay in the end. We met again on the same medical transport flight back to DC. He was a mess, bandages everywhere, but alive. The night we landed, a young girl named Helen had called the Navy asking about Aylmer. She was his high school sweetheart, and they were engaged to be married. She was told she couldn't see him that night but could visit the next day. She and her parents went to the hospital for a bedside reunion. Bob told her that his eye just needed resting and that he'd soon be patched up, good as new. Then he asked Helen for a moment alone with her parents. Aylmer leveled with them about his true condition. In despair over his prognosis, he said that Helen better move on and find somebody else to marry.

Helen soon got the truth from a local paper announcing Bob's return after losing an eye in Korea. She was furious.

"You're not marrying my parents," she told him, "you're marrying me. Anything you can say to them, you can say to me. I can handle it, and I'm not going anywhere."

Bob didn't have any family of his own besides a stepmother who came to the hospital once or twice and never returned, too upset by the sight of him. Helen, on the other hand, was back at his bedside the next day, and the day after that, and every day for many months until he was well enough to be discharged, half blind and unable to walk without pain.

During my time with Bob at Bethesda, I watched men less wounded than him give up to lives of disability checks and self-pity. They didn't have Helen, though. Thanks in no small part to her love, Bob always had enough encouragement to go around.

"Lieutenant Daly,"—for the rest of his days I would try to get him to drop that "Lieutenant" routine—"maybe you can't move those fingers. So what? I saw you hold your baby, that's pretty good. How about I lend you my glass eye so you can roll it around and exercise those fingers?"

His unending drive to rebuild his body shamed and inspired me never to moan about my arm.

A decade passed. In 1962, I was working in the White House when the guard at the Northwest Gate called my office and asked if I knew a man named Bob Aylmer. "He says you saved his life."

"That's not true. He saved his own, but send him in."

We caught up. He was working full time in the State Department and walking the halls, as a messenger, in spite of his shattered knee.

"Lieutenant, I got married."

"That's great, who'd you marry?"

"Who do you think I married?"

Besides being the center of Navy medicine, Bethesda was my hometown. At Sunday family dinners, it could feel like I had never left. But there were times when their worry and pity was all too transparent. A tough moment came when my dad visited the hospital. His own memories must have been welling up as he watched a nurse change the dressing on my arm. At my family's home one afternoon, I was napping on the couch following a big lunch. Ann, the ever-doting, much beloved sister, watched me sleep. She remembers feeling overjoyed her brother was home safe. She went to plant a kiss on my forehead, and the next thing she knew, my fist swung past her head. I was waking up in Korea.

On May 31, 1952, First Lieutenant Charles U. Daly was retired from the United States Marine Corps, as confirmed by these excerpts from the Marine Commandant's letter:

Your disability is permanently related at 40 percent.

I regret that physical conditions necessitate your separation from the active list and wish you many years of happiness and prosperity.

It was time for me to try living a normal life.

THE STICKY ROAD TO THE WHITE HOUSE

1952–1960

"Chuck, your valve-turning days are over."

—JIM FERGUSON, PRESIDENT OF PACIFIC MOLASSES

Pacific Molasses made good on their promise to hold a job for me. The company's president, Jim Ferguson, had learned of my wounding and called the Navy to arrange to meet me during a layover at a military hospital in San Francisco on my way home. We met for lunch. Ferguson said they had no more shipping terminal jobs like the one I had left, but I was to be promoted. He would start me off at their headquarters and possibly have me take responsibility for running the company's twelve scattered terminals across the country.

"In any case, your valve-turning days are over," is how he put it.

We started talking over the phone while I was at Bethesda. Ferguson told me the company could use my help managing their operations in California. That sounded good to me, but I had no idea when I'd be getting out of Bethesda. After I'd spent six months in the Navy's care, Ferguson asked if I could be transferred to the Oak Knoll Naval Hospital in Oakland at Pacific Molasses's expense. The Navy okayed the move, and I started working a few days a week while still in physical therapy. Checking in with my old terminal in Baltimore, I found that Nelson Parker had retired and Pacific Molasses had helped him get his Social Security benefits after they learned that he had lied about his age when he applied for the job because he had been afraid that nobody wanted to hire a fat old black guy. In their fair treatment of Nelson, they won my loyalty.

When I was released from the hospital, I began working full-time and bought a house not far from Pete McCloskey, an hour's commute by train from Palo Alto to San Francisco. Those were happy days, living the California dream of the 1950s, just being alive, and having a family, that now included Douglas. I cringe now when I think that I had a chance to buy a parcel of forty-five inexpensive acres in Napa Valley, now the heart of California Wine Country, with my first bonus. Instead I bought a white two-seater MG convertible, which I crashed into the mailbox in front of Michael's kindergarten.

In early 1957, Ferguson offered to send me to Veracruz, Mexico, where Pacific was struggling to complete a deep-water berth from which molasses from inland sugar mills could be pumped onto ships bound for Europe and our terminals in the eastern United States. As much as I was enjoying life in California, with touch football games, swimming, tennis, hiking, and wonderful new friends, I was still restless. I accepted Ferguson's offer and was appointed vice president of *Mieles de Mexico*. When I arrived in Veracruz, the company was having potentially disastrous welding issues with the giant storage tanks that held the molasses pending shipment. Molasses weighs 11.6 pounds per gallon. Multiply that by over a million gallons in a tank, and you have a deadly tidal wave of heavy syrup if a faulty weld should split. Such a disaster had happened in 1919 in Boston when a molasses tank suffered a stress fracture that made it burst and flooded the streets of the North End resulting in twenty-one gruesome deaths and 150 injuries. To further complicate matters, our partially completed tanks in Veracruz had been damaged in a tropical storm.

I couldn't fire the incompetent welders, because in Mexico a threat to a man's livelihood is a threat to his life and his family. I was told by our local manager that if I fired the welders, one might come back to put a bullet in my head. In light of this unique cultural practice, I saw that incentives were better than threats, so I doubled the welders' wages, providing they would agree to random X-rays of their work to check its soundness and correct minor problems. This was my introduction to the subtle art of bribery that greases the gears of Mexican society. Once we had our terminal nearly built, we needed a pipeline and a pier to connect the tanks to ships that carried molasses overseas. For that we needed the approval of the Mexican Navy, which had been previously promised but was not forthcoming. I went to the secretary of the Navy and was shown the door. Finally, I asked the undersecretary for help. Working with my college Spanish, I made my case.

"*Por Favor, yo quiero hablar con el secretario de* Navy." (I want to speak to the secretary of the Navy.) Roughly translated, I was indicating my willingness to pay a substantial *mordida* (literally, "the bite").

"*No es possible ahora.*" (It's not possible now.)

"*Porque no?*" (Why not?)

"*Muchos ortros negocios hasta tres meses.*" (He's busy for the next three months.)

The project was hung up on a piece of paper. I asked how much it would cost to buy the secretary.

"*Cuanto para comprar el secretario?*"

"*No puedes comprar,*" he replied with indignance, "*pero, se renta...*" (You can't buy him...but you can "rent" him.)

I forget how much I "rented" him for, but it was worth the price. Paying such a bribe was part of ordinary overhead in that part of the world.

Traveling in and out of Mexico City, I would fly first class aboard beautiful four-engine Constellations—in the days of airline food served on tablecloths and wine for everyone, including the pilot and copilot. However, within Mexico and Central America, I took desperate little charter planes. Sometimes the passengers were seated in front of a cargo net, with live farm animals in the back. Nothing eases the fear that you're about to die in turbulence over the mountains like the absurd sight of chickens bouncing around the cargo portion of the cabin. One time, on approach to Veracruz with Ferguson, we hit a flock of birds. When we landed, fuel was leaking out of the wing onto the tarmac. The pilot got out and lit a cigarette. That was Jim's last trip to Mexico.

Beneath the surface of easy living and expat shenanigans, there was real suffering and injustice that people like me played no small part in maintaining and profiting from. A miasma of unfairness hung in the air. One visit to a large sugarcane plantation owned by Erik Koenig stands out. Erik, a German, who had mysteriously appeared in Mexico not long after World War II, not only owned the fields but the town where his workers lived, and more or less possessed all those who lived there and worked for him.

His money bought him the services of a company of the Mexican Army to keep order and do his bidding. Before we left his *hacienda* to tour his holdings, he offered me a *cuarenta y cinco* and opened a case containing two semiautomatic .45 caliber pistols. When I politely declined, he pointed out that we were surrounded by men with machetes who had deep frustrations and little to lose. We were in the nineteenth century. This was slavery. I didn't take a .45, he took his. At lunch that day he returned to the subject of unfairness, saying that the laborers kept making babies. He postulated that the reason they have babies is because they don't have television.

"If they watched TV, they wouldn't fuck so much."

He said this without a hint of cruelty or irony.

★ ★ ★

Mary had tried to join me, but she hated life south of the border. Everything went wrong. The water made her sick. In Mexico City, she had a miscarriage.

By the time I was approaching thirty, I had gotten over the astonishment that I hadn't died at twenty-four. I sensed it was time to do something with this second chance at life, and shipping syrup wasn't it. When I resigned, Ferguson said management was sure I was going over to the competition. I told him I would never do that after all he and the company had done for me, for Nelson Parker, and others. Not content to take me at my word, the higher-ups in London instructed Jim to pay me $1,000 a month for a year to simply stay out of Mexico. I told Ferguson that was generous but unnecessary. He insisted, saying if I didn't take the money, it would confirm London's fear that I would defect to a competitor.

Now I had two boys, one good arm, a disability pension, and my stay-out-of-Mexico money. I had a variety of experience for my age and no financial worries, so like many young men in such a position, I decided to become a writer. It seemed like the best way to do that was to go to journalism school, so I headed to the best J-school in the country, Columbia School of Journalism, the one founded by Mr. Pulitzer himself. In the admissions office, I met with the dean, who walked me through the application process. It was August, and the next class started in less than a month. He suggested I apply for September of the following year.

"That isn't going to work," I told him. "I'm double-parked with my wife and two little boys in the car." Incredibly, I talked myself into the incoming class.

I found a room in the city, in an area where students were warned not to go walking at night.

Just before Christmas, I found a farmhouse in Armonk, New York. I picked up a night job at the *White Plains Reporter Dispatch*. My excitement at seeing my first front page byline was dashed by a typo. My feature about the statue "Christ in Concrete" came back from the press room "*Chris* in Concrete." Trying to cram as much as possible into my budding journalistic résumé, I also did some stringing for the *New York Times* education section. I signed with Sterling Lord, America's top literary agent, who also represented Jack Kerouac. My freelance work included a feature for *Parade* magazine on the Iwo Jima flag raisers and a puff piece on what it's like to be the mother of a high school football player.

Through Eddie Williams, a recent graduate of Columbia, I became interested in The American Political Science Association Congressional Fellowship, which involved spending one half of an academic year with a member of the House and the other half with a senator. In those days, members of Congress made less than some garbage men. Their staffs were small, and staffers were often friends and family, so they welcomed the addition of a potentially useful intern. On the House side, I thought of working with then Congressman Gerald Ford, a nice guy from Michigan. He was a Republican, and I first thought it might be interesting to work with a Democrat and a Republican. Eventually, I chose Democratic Congressman Stewart Udall from Arizona. He was a Mormon with a buzz cut that made him look like a Native American. Udall was an early champion of the environment, endangered species, and water quality. He struck me as bright and interesting. Through Udall, I got involved with the Democratic Study Group (DSG), made up of liberal members of the House who were frustrated that their party was dominated by Southern Democrats and big city mayors like Daley of Chicago and Green of Philadelphia. Udall was backing the Massachusetts Senator Jack Kennedy for President in 1960 and would be involved in the campaign. He suggested I might think about doing my senatorial phase of the internship with Kennedy. When I told him I wasn't particularly interested in Kennedy, Stewart told me he hadn't been either, but he had been won over by the young senator's political skill and their common goals. To say I had no interest in Kennedy was an understatement. His father, Joe, was despised by my family for his support of Hitler while serving as America's ambassador to Britain. Before starting journalism school, I had been working on a scathing satirical novel about Joe Kennedy. When I told my dad about it, he advised against that project.

"I don't think that does anyone any good," he said.

I listened to him and put the manuscript in a bottom drawer.

Good thing I did, because the rest of my life would have gone very differently if I had burned that bridge before it was even in my path.

I took Udall's advice and went with Kennedy for my internship in the Senate. Working for JFK in the spring of 1960 meant working on his presidential primary campaign. We focused on West Virginia. Unemployment in the state was truly awful: oil was replacing coal; handouts were a blow to the pride of these working people. What they wanted was employment, not welfare, not food stamps. Jobs. Jobs. Jobs. Our notes on West Virginia would still apply today, including the deep-seated bigotry that was a problem for the Catholic Kennedy. Mike Feldman, a Kennedy staffer of another faith unfavorable in coal country, once said, "You take a bunch of white protestants and leave them to their own devices, West Virginia is what you get."

In a 1977 oral history, my friend and West Wing staffer, Dick Donahue, described the campaign in West Virginia as,

> "The coldest bath of our lives...I had never heard such open discussion of religious affiliations in my life. And for most of the time we were just constantly beaten over the head by Catholics, protestants, Catholics, protestants, fundamentalists—it was unbelievable."

> Dick had met a cab driver who said he was voting for "the guy running against the Catholic."[9]

There's an iconic picture of Kennedy visiting miners in West Virginia, sitting on a railroad tie wearing a suit. *Listening*. That made an impression, underscoring what Dick Donahue called

---

9   Richard K. Donahue, interview with Bill Hartigan, February 2, 1977 [21-22], John F. Kennedy Library Oral History Program.

candidate Kennedy's "basic fairness." Another icebreaker was the candidate's war record, and, more importantly, that his family was a Gold Star family—like so many in West Virginia. His entire political career had been ordained when his brother, Joseph, the one who had been destined for politics, was killed on a World War II bombing mission. Despite the Kennedy's religion and privilege, his family's sacrifice resonated in a state with more Gold Stars, per capita, than any other in the country.

That's a good story, anyway. But overcoming West Virginia's working class's prejudice mainly meant guys like Dick Donahue canvassing the districts to price sheriffs whom father Joe would pay off. One sheriff asked for $3,000; Joe misheard and sent $30,000. These sheriffs were the seat of local political power in West Virginia. They served single terms and did well for themselves collecting fees from political organizations. Nobody was buying votes per se, but most West Virginians don't work for you on election day unless they're compensated to go to the trouble. You don't pay for their votes, you pay for their gas money to go out and campaign, and they burned a whole lot of gas.

★ ★ ★

Following JFK's victory, the obvious next step for me would have been to try to get a job in his administration. But I didn't see my future in politics. I was a Johnny-come-lately and a protestant. Eligible to travel the world for free with my family on military ships and planes, I found a troop ship leaving the Brooklyn Navy Yard for Hamburg, Germany, and got us two space-available cabins.

I said to the family, "Forget about school this year. We're going to see if I can sell anything as a writer, and if I can't, we're going to have a good time anyway."

As we watched New York slip away in our wake, I said to Mary, "Let's have a drink."

To my horror, we discovered that Navy ships are dry.

Many parched days later, we docked in Hamburg and came ashore to pick up a Volkswagen Beetle we had arranged to buy in advance. We crammed ourselves and our luggage into the tiny car and headed for Spain, which I had only seen in my mind's eye while reading Hemingway.

Driving through Italy, I stopped at an American military base to check our mail. There was a telegram: Dad was dead. He and my mother had moved to Jamaica in search of a climate better suited to his multiple sclerosis. They settled on the North Shore, near Ocho Rios, up the coast from Noel Coward, Ian Fleming, and other less literary Commonwealth expats, exiles, and pensioners. My mother had started walking around with a parrot, named Jeremiah, on her shoulder. Dad would make his way to the water every day for a swim, the sea giving back the ease of movement that had been taken from him on land. His legs had weakened, but he continued to walk with a pair of crutches. He had the heart attack that killed him while seated on a low stool gardening his beloved roses.

Coming home, we went back to California. I got to work again. I handled losing my father the way I had handled Korea. I worked.

After a brief stint at the *San Jose Mercury News*, I got a job at Stanford, where I worked as a copywriter and grant writer translating academic jargon into persuasive copy. The boys loved California and loved not moving around for a change. They made lifelong friends with our neighbors, the Kelleys and the McDonnels.

But it wasn't long before the phone rang with a new job, and I uprooted the boys again. At the time, I didn't think about the impact my restlessness had on my family. I didn't talk to anyone about joining the Marine Corps or about making sure the Corps sent me to Korea. I never consulted Mary or the boys on any of our moves. On at least one occasion, they came home from school to find their stuff packed. Moving into one new house, Michael climbed up on the roof and declared, "I'm never moving again."

Looking back, I can't change history, but I can acknowledge my selfishness in retelling it.

A BORROWED UNIFORM

1961

"202-456-1414"

—WHITE HOUSE PHONE NUMBER

I was in the shower when Mary told me someone claiming to be from the White House was on the line. I figured it was McCloskey making a prank call and asked her to take the number and hang up.

After my shower and breakfast, I rang the number the caller left with Mary. A White House operator put me through to Larry O'Brien, head of President Kennedy's congressional liaison staff, who said they were adding someone to the team and asked me if I would consider coming aboard.

"There's no better job here but mine and the president's," he said, "and we need you yesterday."

I asked Larry if I could get back to him tomorrow.

Unlike my decision to go to war, I talked this one over with Mary, and this time, I had her enthusiastic support. I called Larry back and told him to expect me by the end of the week. I advised my boss at Stanford, Ken Cuthbertson, of my decision.

"Do it. If it doesn't work out, come back here."

I said my goodbyes to our friends and neighbors and borrowed a uniform from a Marine down the street who had been a Corsair pilot. The uniform and my ID. got me a free space-available flight from Naval Air Station, Mountain View, California, to NAS Memphis. From there I bought a bus ticket to Washington, DC.

* * *

I rented a room near the Capitol, and the next morning, splurged on a cab down to the old State Department Building, now the Executive Office Building. I told a guard that Larry O'Brien was expecting me.

"Not here he isn't. Try next door at the Northwest Gate."

The Northwest Gate...of the White House. The guard there made a call, and then told me I'd find O'Brien on the second floor. No escort, just a finger pointed up the driveway to the door of the two-story West Wing of the mansion.

Inside the marbled lobby, a small woman was waiting.

"Hi. I'm Phyllis Maddox, Mr. O'Brien's secretary. Please come with me." We walked through the lobby into a hallway. "The president's office is in there, just past Kenny O'Donnell's desk. We're upstairs."

Phyllis led me up to a large office, where Larry was sitting behind his desk in a cloud of cigarette smoke. On a sofa and chairs around his desk were four men whom I was about to learn were Kennedy's congressional liaison team, my new teammates. These guys were Kennedy's political infantry. Our job was to help generate congressional will and votes for JFK's bold promises, from civil rights to the moon landing.

Larry O'Brien gave introductions: "Mike Manatos handles the Senate side of things, Henry Hall Wilson 'Molasses Mouth,' a former state senator from North Carolina, handles the South. Claude Desautels is our 'inside man.'" By that, I would learn, Larry meant he wasn't let out of the White House.

"Dick Donahue does the big cities."

Dick interrupted the orientation and turned to me. "That leaves all those liberal cocksuckers, they're yours." He was referring to the more liberal members of Congress. "We're discussing Weaver and how to get a colored guy confirmed into the cabinet."

I took a seat in a single empty chair.

O'Brien turned to the guys. "There's no problem with setting up a Department of Urban Affairs, the problem is Weaver."

Weaver was then the head of Housing and Home Finance (HHFA). He was a symbol of black progress. The problem was the president had announced his intention to appoint a "colored" guy to his cabinet before he had the necessary funding from Congress. This was a bold move in a time when many congressmen didn't want "colored" men to do anything on the Hill but clean toilets.

When Larry ended the meeting, he turned to me. "Phyllis will show you to your office. Go get set up, and give Congressman Dan Flood a call to see if he's okay on this one..."

Phyllis led me down the hall, pointing out the other staff offices. We turned into a vast corner office facing Pennsylvania Avenue, furnished with a fine desk, a leather sofa, and two big chairs.

"This is you."

"Nice space. What did I do to deserve it?"

"It used to be Dick Goodwin's. He doesn't need it anymore," she replied and exited with a conspiratorial little smile.

I had dealt with Goodwin when I was interning in Senator Kennedy's office, where he had been difficult. What I didn't know at the time was that Goodwin had been Mr. Impossible in the White House. He was extraordinarily bright and never let anyone forget that fact. He had little interest in being helpful to Kenny, Larry, or anyone but himself. Goodwin was an expert on Latin America, and Kenny figured his skillset might be put to better use outside the White House and occasionally in the Southern Hemisphere. Following Goodwin's departure, they recognized the dangers of a vacuum, so they filled it with me.

My first task was to call Congressman Dan Flood. Who the hell was Dan Flood? I had no recollection of him from the Democratic Study Group. Fortunately, I found a Congressional Directory with brief bios and photographs on an otherwise empty bookshelf.

> "Daniel J. Flood, from Wilkes Barre, PA had been in and out of Congress, losing and regaining his seat a couple times."

I picked up the phone. An operator said, "Yes, Mr. Daly, can I help you?"

"Do you have Congressman Flood's number?"

"I'll get him on the line and call you right back."

Big mistake. As I was about to learn, congressmen don't like to be held on the line to await a call from a flunky, not even a White House flunky.

Two minutes later: "This is Dan Flood."

"Hello, Congressman. I'm Chuck Daly. I'm the new guy on Larry O'Brien's staff. I look forward to working with you."

"Well, congratulations, Mr. Daly. And what might your title be?"

"Staff Assistant to the President for Congressional Relations."

"My, that's impressive. And what can I do for you?"

"Well, I just wanted to say 'hello' and ask if you'll vote with the president on the Urban Affairs bill."

"Sonny, presidents don't have a vote up here. And you can tell Larry that this time he does not have mine. Goodbye, *Mr. Daly.*"

Ouch.

Not long after that unfortunate call, a Member from New Jersey, Frank Thompson, whom I had known from the DSG, gave me some advice on how to conduct myself.

"Chuck, can I give you a tip? The White House operator can find anyone in the world, and that's good when the president is on the line. But if the operator calls and Chuck Daly is on the line, it's different. If you personally call as 'Chuck Daly from O'Brien's office,' my office will put you on hold. If I'm there and feel like talking, I'll get on the line. Those extra minutes you spend will go a long way toward not only getting a vote but building a relationship."

My young ego would get another challenge when I ran into General David M. Shoup, 22nd Commandant of the Marine Corps, on his way to a meeting of the Joint Chiefs of Staff. I introduced myself as the only Marine on Kennedy's staff.

"Good," he said, "and what have you done for your country lately?"

Looking back, Shoup's words remind me how much I owe President Kennedy. More than the corner office and an impressive item on my résumé, he gave me a way to serve my country without a weapon in my hands. Those words stung at the time, but I've never forgotten Shoup's challenge. I ask myself that question today as an old man sitting on my ass writing my memoir.

The president himself gave a powerful lesson on when not to use the White House telephone. There was a wonderful guy, Clem Miller, running for a normally Republican district north of the Golden Gate Bridge. He was so wonderful that he still won the election after having died in a plane crash while campaigning. There would be a special election. Clem had been against the inheritance of seats by House widows and so was his widow Katherine, who stood to inherit his. The seat was important given our narrow margin in Congress. But Katherine couldn't be persuaded, not by me anyway. At Larry's suggestion, I made the pitch to the president in the Oval Office. I acknowledged the considerations about Katherine's young children and her views on inherited seats.

"The only way to hold that seat is if she runs, and the only way she is going to run is if you call her."

After hearing me out, the president said, "There goes that district."

★ ★ ★

One morning, I dropped into Dick Donahue's office where he was finishing up a phone call. Here's what I heard on his end:

"I don't care who told you that."

...

"That's bullshit."

...

"Hey, do what you want."

End of conversation. Dick cradled the phone, turned to me, and said, "Just because he's the president doesn't mean everyone around him is supposed to kiss his ass."

"Jesus. How long have you known each other?"

"Twenty or so years, but I never had to work for him before."

Dick had been there from the start. He had met his wife, Nancy, on one of Kennedy's campaigns.

"Dick, I want to ask you about Weaver and Flood..."

"Flood's from a tough town in Pennsylvania, and Weaver's colored. What else is there to know? Flood is a probable 'no,' but he might be okay if he's needed. No guarantee."

"Any suggestions for me?"

"Get up to the Hill and pound the halls. Shake a lot of hands before you ask for anything. Get their constituents on the special White House tour list. If you have to twist an arm, remember we'll want the guy on another vote on another bill tomorrow. Don't twist too hard. Reward him when he's right. You've got a handle on every agency, so you can do all kinds of favors."

"I've marked up this directory with the names I know at least a little and the ones I don't. Can you tell me something about the strangers?"

"Sure. Ashley: Good guy, hot temper, from Toledo.

"Fisk: a California Okie. Pain in the ass, but a good vote. That whole California delegation isn't organized like Chicago, but mostly they'll all vote okay. But ask each one each time all the same.

"Rostenkowski: That's Chicago. Say hello and get acquainted, but let Kenny handle him until you get to know him. He's smart enough to know that while he's a big man in DC, he's just Daley's puppet in Chicago."

This, by the way, may have been my first hint of Mayor Daley's omnipotence in that town. A force I would later encounter firsthand.

"McCormack: The new Speaker's no Rayburn, but he's not a dummy. Nothing in his life but his wife Harriet and the House. Kennedys make him nervous because he's from Massachusetts and they don't always have a handle on him. Watch out for McCormack's guy Martin Swieg...he peddles access.

"Albert: The mighty midget from Oklahoma. McCormack's number two and a good guy. Future Speaker.

"Hale Boggs: The Majority Whip, the vote counter who can't count. New Orleans through and through. Drink his sauce, but don't rely on his numbers."

Congressman Frank Thompson, New Jersey (left), Congressman Phil Burton, California (center), and me (right).

A SMALL MARGIN

1961–1963

"All this will not be finished in the first one hundred days. Nor will it be finished in the first one thousand days, not in the life of this Administration, nor even perhaps in our lifetime on this planet. But let us begin."

—JFK, INAUGURAL ADDRESS

Kennedy had only narrowly won the election. Once sworn in, he faced obstructionism by Republicans and Southern Democrats, a hostile Congress, and a national mood that had been slow to embrace his promises of a vigorous set of challenges, having spent the 1950s lulled in the dull safety of Eisenhower conservatism.

In a conversation with Kenny O'Donnell at the Democratic National Convention, candidate Kennedy had expressed concern about the Senate in terms of his choice of a vice president. He told O'Donnell that his good health meant he would not die in office, and so his choice of a VP was strictly a political move. As Kenny later wrote,

> "If we win, it will be by a small margin and I won't be able to live with Johnson as the leader of a small majority in the Senate. Did it occur to

you that if Lyndon becomes Vice President, I'll have Mike Mansfield as the leader in the Senate, somebody I can trust and depend on?"[10]

Kennedy was keenly aware of Johnson's power and that of the Southern Democrats.

"If Johnson and Rayburn leave here (the Convention) mad at me, they'll ruin me in Congress...I'll be the laughingstock of the country. Nixon will say I haven't any power in my own party, and I'll lose the election before Labor Day. So, I've got to make peace now with Johnson and Rayburn, and offering Johnson the vice presidency, whether he accepts it or not, is one way of keeping him friendly until Congress adjourns...All of this is more important to me than Southern votes, which I won't get anyway with the Catholic thing working against me. I doubt if Lyndon will even be able to carry Texas."[11]

JFK was known for his charm and charisma, but he had an insecure side. I encountered this sensitivity firsthand in early 1963 while working with Wayne Phillips, of the DNC, who kept tabs on dozens of right-wing radio broadcasts and worked on developing a system to get equal time to respond. The president became interested in what those programs had to say about him. On one occasion, I told the president about a drive-time radio show I had listened to that morning that likened him to a Communist and speculated on the state of his health.

"Who listens to that crap?" he asked me.

---

10 Kenneth P. O'Donnell and David F. Powers, *Johnny, We Hardly Knew Ye*.

11 O'Donnell and Powers, *Johnny*.

"A lot of people like myself, Mr. President, driving to work—some just spinning the dial, and others selling the gospel."[12]

That's me on the right.

12 Charles U. Daly, interview with Charles T. Morrissey, April 5, 1966 [10-12], John F. Kennedy Library Oral History Program.

Kennedy's youth had won over many voters, but from a legislative point of view, it was a weakness and liability. Most Democratic congressmen had received more votes in their home districts than Kennedy had. At first, they were reluctant to risk losing reelection by backing an unproven president. As liaisons to the Congress, O'Brien and his staff faced what Dick Donahue described as "a long persuasion job." Gradually, we did our part to help turn Congress's 50 percent or so following of the administration to something more like 60 or 70 percent, according to Dick's somewhat rosy analysis.

When we needed help on a vote, Larry would get me a potentially helpful Member into the Oval Office, where the president romanced our guest for a few minutes. I would mention a bill, at which point the president would appeal for the support we needed and talk about what the bill would mean across the country and what the benefit would be many years from now. On one occasion, a congressman from Colorado whom we needed to vote on a water project became our greatest cheerleader for the bill, touting the benefits to Massachusetts and Illinois and "even Georgia," parroting the president's own words about a congressman willing to stick his neck out for something bigger than the short-term interests of his own district.

This is where the legend of JFK doesn't begin to convey his political skill. Some historians have described him as a relatively weak legislative leader but a great philosophical man, an idea guy, a man of principles but not tactics or strategy. He was an idea guy, but he was also a highly effective legislative leader. During his too brief time in the White House, he and his legislative team lead the Congress to create: the Peace Corps and the SEAL Teams, the Alliance for Progress, Medicare, The Model Cities Program, the Nuclear Test Ban Treaty, increased aid to education, and the foundation for the historic 1964 Civil Rights Act. The tragedy of his unfinished first term and unrealized second was not the death of a set of ideals or a dream for the nation—those didn't die—but massive setbacks in terms of the ground game of representative politics. What we lost was not just a visionary who literally promised us the moon, but a statesman who achieved a legislative mandate and united action for political ideas that had seemed like moonshots of their own.

We were hyperconscious of the president's narrow margin of victory and slim mandate, or lack of a mandate, coming out of 1960. We needed him to be needed in 1964. We had to show that Kennedy's agenda was in the interest of representatives who were reluctant to enmesh their reputations with his.

Not that Kenny or Larry or Dick or I had a free moment to consider the larger implications of our work...Dick described working in Kennedy's West Wing as "the most thrilling experience you could have." He and I were earning around $13,000 a year. Our work wasn't a résumé builder, a stopgap, or a rung on some ladder. These were the days before the scumbagification of Washington. We weren't setting ourselves up for futures in consulting or lobbying. Our joy and sole motive was to serve the president and his ideals. Our work depended on our individual contacts within each of the major cabinet operations, where we empowered one or two persons to come to the White House for group discussions of how best to coordinate and advance the president's objectives. O'Brien's five-man team was lean, and we got things done.

It's fitting that O'Donnell's book is dedicated "to our wives, for their many sacrifices."

Dick's wife, Nancy Donahue, remembers, "Our husbands worked

government jobs, like everyone else on our block, and we never saw them."

She remembers those days as a blur.

"I'd give him his coffee and toast, the car came, and he'd go. He was home after the kids went to bed."

Nancy and Dick had six children when they came down from Lowell, Massachusetts. Number seven was born while he was in the West Wing, and Nancy was pregnant with their eighth, of a final eleven, when they returned to Lowell in 1963.

When Dick decided to leave the White House and return to Massachusetts to resume his law practice, the president invited him to bring the family to work so he could say goodbye. Sadly, the president's own new baby son, Patrick, died the week before that meeting, so Kenny pulled the Donahues from the schedule out of sensitivity. When the president noticed the change, he instructed Kenny to restore the appointment.

While the Donahues were waiting to see the president, their youngest crawled under a table in the waiting room and wouldn't come out from under it when they went into the Oval Office. Dick picked up the baby, who immediately began to cry.

The president said, "Give the baby to Nancy; you can tell he doesn't know who you are."

★ ★ ★

On one of my trips down the halls of the Capitol, I first met Thomas Ludlow "Lud" Ashley from Toledo, Ohio, grandson of the Congressman Ashley who put in the papers to impeach President Johnson—*Andrew* Johnson—and coauthored the Thirteenth Amendment to abolish slavery. I had not expected my first meeting with Lud to go well, because I was carrying bad news. A federal arsenal in his district was being shut down, taking many jobs with it. I needed to tell him that and then shamelessly ask for his vote on another issue.

"Congressman, I know this is one hell of a way to pay back your constant loyalty to the president..."

He cut me off. "So that's what I get for being an easy vote. Well, you don't have to worry about me on a tough vote, because there's a man in your office named Richard K. Donahue."

"I don't know why, but thank you."

"Sit down, and I'll tell you why..."

Before I met Lud, Dick was having some preinaugural drinks at a party paid for by Ambassador Joe Kennedy. Donahue got talking with some congressmen, including Lud. Dick had heard that Lud's father had fallen earlier that day and was now at Bethesda Naval Hospital with a broken hip and a hangover.

"Hey, Mr. Ludlow Ashley, I hear your dad's going to miss the inaugural because he got pissed and busted his ass."

"Well, Mr. Whoever You Are, fuck you. You want to take this outside?"

When I launched into an apology and some ass kissing, Lud cut me off again.

"Let me finish...Earlier that morning, through heavy snow and ice, a Marine, clad in dress blues and white gloves, made his way to my dad's bedside at Bethesda, saluted, and handed him an envelope with a letter that read:

Dear Mr. Ashley,

I was very sorry to hear of your unfortunate accident. I've attached an advanced copy of my inaugural address. I hope you will find it to be of some interest.

You have my best wishes for a speedy recovery.

S/ John F. Kennedy

"So, tell Larry and your pal Donahue that I won't scream about the arsenal."

"Jesus, that's a hell of a story. How 'bout a drink?"

"Let's go."

Thus began a close friendship that would last the rest of his life and nearly cost me mine on the occasions that Lud took me flying. In his spare time, Lud was a pilot who was short on skill but long on enthusiasm and luck. I once watched him nearly fly through the screen of a drive-in movie theater with my boys onboard. On the morning of November 22, 1963, he rented a plane and flew it to Hyannis to spend the weekend with his father. Upon landing, he heard the terrible news and sat down with his dad and a bottle of Johnnie Walker Black.

About a week later, he called me. "I got a problem. The plane rental people want to know where their plane is. I don't know where the fucking plane is, but I put down a deposit."

I managed to track down the plane and protect his pilot's license while I was at it.

Lud and I had Yale in common, though he had been a man of quality and heritage who attended as a matter of good breeding, not by the grace of the G.I. Bill. One time we were at dinner with our pal, the future Speaker Tip O'Neill, who wanted to ask two Yale guys what goes on at Skull & Bones. Lud, a member of this secret and powerful order, was sworn to uphold the mysteries surrounding the society. But I was far from Skull & Bones material and was bound by no such vow. When Tip asked, I told him I knew exactly what goes on there.

"Chuck, tell me."

"They get together on Friday nights in that big windowless concrete building in New Haven and unzip their pants and sit in a circle and each man grabs the penis of the man to his right and they tell secrets."

Tip was horrified.

"Ludlow! Is this true? Did you do that with George Bush?"

"Daly, you son of a bitch. I am going to kill you!"

★ ★ ★

Kennedy had appointed my old boss, Stewart Udall, as Secretary of the Interior. His open seat was won by his brother, Mo, the thrice-married, one-eyed grandson of a polygamist Mormon. I liked Mo, and we spent many hours together during and long after my White House days. A would-be Speaker and president, he was foiled in the first instance by the fact that he was reform-minded and in the second by an underfinanced and mismanaged primary campaign against Jimmy Carter.

After his second-place finish, I remember him quipping, "The people have spoken. The bastards!"

Mo would befriend dozens of other Members on both sides of the aisle over the years, including a war hero freshman Republican named John McCain. During Mo's final years, when he was wasting away from the advanced stages of Parkinson's, McCain routinely came to his bedside at Walter Reed to read books to his eventually unresponsive friend.

★ ★ ★

Much of my education in the power games of Congress happened at Paul Young's, a large basement restaurant opposite the Mayflower Hotel. The place had taken off after old Joe Kennedy rented the entire establishment for a preinauguration party, the one at which Lud and Dick had words.

By invitation, I became a regular at the table of powerful congressmen and senators. The table itself, a round one located strategically at the bottom of the entry stairs with room for around eight or ten, had been secured by Michael Kirwan, a powerhouse who once found the table occupied and threatened to never return and to blacklist the place, which would have been disastrous for the owners. To rectify this, Paul Young put up a plaque permanently reserving the table for Kirwan.

Ed Kane, the only lobbyist allowed at the table, would pick up the tab. Ed was not allowed to talk. Nevertheless, I'm sure his employer, the Delaware Racing Commission, was happy to see lunch with these names on the expense account.

This was where deals got done to help bills that wouldn't hurt one's own reelection chances in exchange for others' support on other matters. Of all the bits of wisdom I gleaned from those dinners, one that would later prove invaluable to me was an offhand comment about Chicago politics. One evening, Michael Kirwan allowed Danny Rostenkowski, a senior member of the House and a key member of the Ways and Means Committee, to bring Chicago Alderman Matt Danaher to the table.

The condescending congressman from New York, Eugene James Keogh, asked, "Now, Mr. Alderman, tell us, what exactly does an alderman do in Chicago?"

Danaher answered, "Well, Congressman, I don't know what an alderman does in New York, but I know that in Chicago, a congressman carries the alderman's bags. Isn't that right, Danny?"

"Yes."

Any House member from Chicago was doomed if an alderman close to Mayor Daley got on his case.

Looking towards 1964, we knew it was vital to get the historic civil rights bill out of the Judiciary Committee even without support of Southern Democrats. I asked Jim Corman, a Marine veteran of Iwo Jima who represented an ultraliberal Southern California district, to vote on a bill that wasn't as strong as what his constituents demanded.

"Chuck, I've got a close race, and this vote could kill me. Can't you see who else you can get?"

Then I asked Don Edwards, a new Member from an equally liberal but safe district in California.

Edwards said, "I can't do it. I can't vote to get that bill out of committee, it's just too weak."

"You *can* do it, but you say you *won't* do it."

Faced with Edwards's refusal, and accepting my judgment that moving the bill was a vital step toward enactment, Corman promised to vote our way.

Throughout these discussions, I had counted on Chicago's Libonati voting the right way, since he did what Daley said, and Daley was with us on this one. But the idiot blindsided me by voting *against*, and so the bill was sent back to committee even with Corman's very public vote. I went to Kenny, who was close to Daley.

"Libonati just blew the fucking bill out of the fucking water. It's going to cost Corman his seat."

"Okay," Kenny said, "leave it with me."

The next day, on the floor of the House, Libonati came to Rostenkowski, with tears in his eyes.

"Danny, they told me I can't be a congressman anymore."

"Who told you that?"

He whispered a name, probably a boss out of Chicago's notorious First Ward. Like something out of *The Godfather*, Danny shook the doomed congressman's hand and said, "Libby, you've had a great career."

As a consolation prize, former congressman Roland Victor Libonati got to walk at the head of Chicago's next Columbus Day parade.

★ ★ ★

I have a framed poster from the JFK Library. The caption reads, *It's okay to smile.*

The photo depicts JFK Jr. as a toddler, crawling under the president's desk, a big smile on his face. The rest of the image is taken up by a semicircle of men with serious faces, cabinet officers meeting with their equally serious-looking president. A bit apart, with the child between him and the circle, Kenny O'Donnell stands alone, his fingers curled in front of his mouth in a gesture of intense concentration. His eyes are on the president. That was Kenny, as always, tough and intensely focused. Perhaps thinking of a response for the president when asked for his thoughts on the meeting.

O'Donnell had no social life, not even with his family. Kennedy was his life. But if that quality made him difficult, it also made him astonishingly effective. He could be funny, but funny in a Kenny way that is impossible to describe, like a very dry inside joke.

He had been a bombardier over Europe in the war, earning a Distinguished Flying Cross. He had gone to Harvard on the G.I. Bill.

Kenny acted as a gatekeeper with a desk in the reception area just outside the president's door. He writes, "We had to limit and protect him from unwelcome intruders, time-wasting well-wishers and small-talkers and other appointment-schedule wreckers."[13] And it was that last type, the time-wasters and schedule-wreckers, that Kenny had a special gift for blocking. Sometimes this meant arguing with the president over the value of a given visit. Kenny writes of one instance when the president told him to schedule a guy who wanted to drop in and say hello. Kenny pointed out that the fellow in question had a personal stake in a bill that was coming up.

"Is that so?" the president replied. "I thought he just wanted a social visit. Tell him I'm too busy."[14]

It would drive Kenny crazy when someone would go around him. In one such instance, Postmaster Ed Day persuaded the president's personal secretary to let him into the Oval Office through her door. Day was in the middle of telling the president a joke when Kenny walked in and stood with his arms crossed, wordlessly staring. Postmaster General Day forgot the punchline.

Another time Kenny came to me laughing the morning after he and the president had been on a trip.

"You won't believe this one."

General Clifton, the Army aide to the president, frequently complained that he wasn't onboard Marine One on trips, or at least in the next chopper behind it. The general came to Kenny's hotel

---

13 O'Donnell and Powers, *Johnny*.

14 O'Donnell and Powers, *Johnny*.

room to air his grievance. Kenny had left the connecting door between his room and Kennedy's suite slightly ajar so the president could hear their conversation.

When Clifton departed, the president said, "Jesus, Kenny, that must have been General MacArthur you were talking to."

Russell Long was an old-time, semihonest senator from Louisiana. Once we needed his vote, but he was a "no." At Larry's suggestion, Kenny got him on *Honey Fitz,* the presidential yacht, for a cruise on the Potomac. For the first hour, Kenny poured booze into the ever-thirsty senator before getting to the point.

"We gotta have this vote, you gonna be all right?"

"Okay. Okay. I'm gonna be all right."

The next morning, Kenny urged the president to call Long right away and thank him for promising to be okay on the bill.

"I'll be okay on this one, Mr. President, but it was that goddamned Kenny. He got me drunk, but I ain't no liar."

Kenny epitomized the old proverb "revenge is a dish best served cold." It was Kenny's cool temper that taught me to at least attempt to control mine in a situation where I was ready to walk out the door.

Postmaster Day was succeeded by John A. Gronouski. We had a bill that Congressman Kastenmeire, from Madison, Wisconsin, voted against for no real reason. He was in a safe district, a liberal university town. It made no sense. I put word out that we're not to go out of our way to approve anything for that particular congressman anytime soon. A few days later, Gronouski announced that there would be a new post office in Kastenmeire's district. What the hell was that all about?

It turns out Gronouski, who was also from Wisconsin, wanted to help his pal Kastenmeire, so he gave him a post office. I wrote a letter and had it handed to the postmaster to let him know that his actions were not appreciated. After being shown my note, Congressman Kastenmeire took to the floor of the House to make remarks, on the record, about the arrogance of young persons in the West Wing.

I went to Kenny and said, "I'm going down there to punch that cocksucker in the mouth and that will be the end of my illustrious career, and I don't give a damn."

Kenny told me to hold my fire. "One day Gronouski will walk into a revolving door spinning the wrong way, and it's going to smack him right in the face..."

Nearly two years later, Kenny would deliver on that promise as one of his last acts in Washington.

WE DON'T DO PEARL HARBORS

OCTOBER 1962

"In the nuclear age, superpowers make war like porcupines make love—carefully."

—ROBERT F. KENNEDY

Leading up to the '62 midterm elections, we still had a weak margin in the House. We were heading into partisan battles hoping to add some seats. Larry and I thought we should spread some money around out West. He sent me out there with a briefcase containing $55,000 cash—from the Democratic National Committee. To work the Senate side, Mike Manatos came along with similar luggage, though not as much of it. It's not easy to sway a senator, but it didn't hurt to be friendly.

Meanwhile, there had been rumors of a Soviet buildup in Cuba, but these had been dismissed as GOP scare tactics. Unbeknownst to me, in a darkroom at the CIA's National Photo Interpretation Center (NPIC), located in a nondescript building at Fifth and K in Washington, my brother-in-law, John Hicks, the man who had inspired me to join the Marines and had gone from the Corps to the CIA, was analyzing film from an American spy plane that clearly showed missiles in Cuba, ninety miles from our coast. The photos indicated at least six canvas-covered missile trailers, about seventy-five vehicles, eight small tents, and some buildings under construction—in other words, a launch site at or near the operational stage. Another set of images showed several more missiles.[15] John later told me that upon realizing what he was looking at, he proceeded to smoke a half-dozen Camels before an analysis was sent to the White House. My sister Joan never knew any of this. She preferred not to ask her husband about his work, fearful she'd talk after a couple of martinis.

While this was going on, Manatos and I were in California distributing our gifts. On October 16, Larry called us. He had no idea what was going on, but he knew something was up and instructed Manatos to check in to The Beverly Hills Hotel, sit tight, and hold on to any remaining cash. Shortly thereafter, two beautiful ladies appeared at our door, sent by Jesse Unruh, boss of the California Democrats. Worried about leaks, and distracted by our own bewilderment as to what was going on back in Washington, we weren't in the mood for romance.

"Thanks, but no thanks, girls."

Later that night, Larry called to brief us on what little he knew about the situation, which was enough to get us on the next flight out. The first thing I did in DC was return the money.

Friends and family assume I must have had inside knowledge of this critical moment in history. But only the dozen members of the president's ExComm, who were directly involved in dis-

---

15   Ernest R. May and Philip D. Zelikow (Eds), *The Kennedy Tapes: Inside the White House During the Cuban Missile Crisis*, 48.

cussing the military situation, were aware of the details. It was strictly need-to-know.

On October 22, I listened to the president's speech on the eve of a possible nuclear holocaust. Like every parent in America, I thought of my family. Looking back, it's comforting to know that the man with his finger on the button had the same worries, as Kennedy's many hours of secretly recorded tapes indicate.

Unlike some of the hawks advising him, Kennedy had a personal experience of war that put military intervention in human terms. In a letter to his father in World War II, he wrote:

> "People get so used to talking about billions of dollars and millions of soldiers that thousands of dead sounds like drops in the bucket. But if those thousands want to live as much as the ten I saw (on PT-109)—they should measure their words with great, great care."[16]

By contrast, General Curtis LeMay, who advised the president and his ExCOMM in those tense days in October, had only known war from that great distance that the president spoke of. As a commander of bombers, LeMay had been removed, by altitude, from the realities of violence.

LeMay told the president, "We don't have any choice but military action," and that he wanted to do "more than take out the missiles," saying that the success of an airstrike was "a guarantee."

The general rejected any alternatives to military intervention and couched his arguments in personal, threatening terms, empha-

---

16   O'Donnell and Powers, *Johnny*, 5.

sizing that the president would appear "pretty weak" to the world if he didn't strike.

"*You're* in a pretty bad fix, Mr. President."

"What did you say?"

"You're in a pretty bad fix."

The transcript of the tapes indicates that Kennedy rejected the threat by making an "unclear joking reply."

Bobby Kennedy, though he had been vicious on Cuba, told the generals, "We don't do Pearl Harbors."

★ ★ ★

"Bombs Away" LeMay, as he was known, was perverse about his antiseptic brand of killing. He bragged about firebombing civilians in Japan during World War II. During the Korean War, he spoke of "deleting" cities and later complained to all who would listen that the war could have been won cleanly and quickly if only he'd been allowed to firebomb the major cities in China. He spoke of war in terms of cost-benefit analysis and embraced nukes as the next big thing in killing, something like the microwave oven of murder: the newest, quickest, and oh-so-space-age way of getting it done. There is no bottom to my contempt for this man and those like him.

In my war, I was grateful for the air support that protected my Marines, but I never forgot that those pilots and the generals who sent them would never see or smell the bodies they barbecued as we on the ground had. The South Koreans had a nickname for

US Marine infantry. They called us "ghost thieves" because we were so fearsome that we stole the ghosts of the men we killed. They couldn't know how true this is. Those ghosts are inside me still. They will never leave me. When I draw my last breath, the woman and the child in the photograph belonging to the North Korean I killed will be right there with the faces of my own children and the women I married. It can't possibly be the same for a bombardier for whom taking a life means traveling to a set of coordinates while seated in a cockpit, pushing a button, and turning for home. Or, nowadays, from a computer screen in Colorado guiding a drone strike.

TAPS

NOVEMBER 1963

"...we'll never be young again."

—DANIEL PATRICK MOYNIHAN

In my office that November 22, after the news came in from Dallas, I wondered how to talk to Michael and Douglas about it. The White House had been a place of wonder to them. They had been so grossly cheated by the loss of this man.

I wandered down to the Mess, to a meal served in silence. One of the stewards was weeping. He arranged my silverware with shaking hands.

The galley ran out of sirloin steaks.

I forced down what I had ordered and resumed drinking endless ice teas.

Walking aimlessly down the halls with glass in hand, I ran into Kennedy's speechwriter, Ted Sorensen. He said something about Communists.

"Ted, what if this wasn't any great conspiracy, just a nobody?"

A total guess that later turned out to be true.

Back in my office, the phone rang. The operator's normally impersonal voice seemed to tremble as she delivered a collection of phone messages I wasn't planning to answer.

I thought about joining a group heading to Andrews Air Force Base to greet the body and the new president. What good would that have done? I thought of the old and new suck-asses around Johnson, now President Johnson, and decided to give that tour a pass. I closed the door to my office and stretched out on the sofa. Around six in the evening, the TV showed Johnson and Mrs. Kennedy standing on the forklift platform lowering the box to the tarmac and a waiting ambulance destined for Bethesda Naval Hospital for an autopsy.

Admiral Burkley, the president's doctor—who, in his spare time, had not only removed my son Michael's appendix but brought it out to show me how close it had been to bursting—would have to watch as they examined Kennedy's shattered skull and then tried to paste the bits and pieces together.

I had seen the results of what a bullet does to a skull. I knew what it was like to wear clothes splattered with blood and brain matter. I'd seen David Ivens's head and smiling face intact one moment and fragmented all over me the next. I handled the sight at the time. I handled it until that November night a dozen years later. I was finally feeling it. I had mortgaged my trauma and now it was all due with interest.

I would later learn that Jackie, even in the shock of her grief, had also fixated on the gore and the grim specifics of close contact with a headshot. Her closest friend, Bunny Mellon, remembers their conversation in her memoir:

"She (Jackie) needed to talk about what had happened in Dallas, describing what it was like to be by her husband's side when shots exploded and he was hit in the head, blood and tissue splattering everywhere. Jackie said her instinctive reaction was to 'put it back.'"[17]

When I saw Jackie's bloodstained outfit on television, I saw my own splattered fatigues.

I exchanged repeated calls with Mary. Late that night, I went downstairs and walked out onto the grass beyond the Rose Garden, where the night was still and peaceful.

I looked back at the rear of the West Wing, all lit up as if for a party. I moved onto the portico and the walkway between the tall pillars and the glass doors of President Kennedy's office. So empty. My colleague, Henry Hall Wilson, was there, tall and quiet. We stood for a while but didn't speak. In the distance, a bulb from an unseen camera flashed. I slumped back into the building.

17 Meryl Gordon, *Bunny Mellon: The Life of an American Style Legend*.

The White House from the Rose Garden, November 22, 1963. Me, far left, with my head down.

I went to Kenny O'Donnell's desk and saw nervous LBJ guys standing there at the door to the Oval Office. Three of them not yet inside but already in a place they'd never seen. I stared, silent, unable to return kind words. They left.

Upstairs, I asked the operator to get me Kenny at the hospital.

"Tough world, Kenny."

"None tougher."

"Some shitheads are sniffing around your desk. Anything I should do?"

"Get my [rosary] beads and the FBI files out of the bottom drawer."

I carried the folders upstairs and sat with those beads in my hand. I had never held rosary beads, and I didn't know any Catholic prayers. But no amount of mumbo jumbo would do any good. Then there were the files. *The Files.* JFK's FBI files. I knew Kenny regularly read Hoover's gossip on real or imagined scandals. I hadn't known he'd been shortstopping poisonous, potentially compromising files.

"The president wants us to know about men who screw boys not girls," he once told Edgar, relaying that gem to me with a rare smile.

At about 4:00 a.m., a guard called to say the hearse was headed in from Bethesda. I secured the files in my desk drawer, still unread as they would remain until I handed them back to Kenny, and went down to the Northwest Gate.

A squad of riflemen in dress uniforms slow-stepped in front of the motorcade escorting the Navy ambulance carrying Kennedy onto the grounds. One guard stood by the gate's pedestal, hands behind his back, eyes fixed on the slow-moving procession of vehicles.

I went ahead to look at the East Room. It was being decked out with black drapes. I left and just continued pacing. An hour or so later, I went back. The casket had been placed atop a two-tiered black platform flanked by an honor guard and priests.

In the morning, I called home. Poor Douglas, now ten years old, had, on November 13 served, for the first time, as a White House usher. Per Jackie's instruction, the little ushers were treated to a spaghetti lunch sitting on the floor on an elegant carpet in the East Wing.

Earlier that month, I had taken the boys to work on a Saturday. We were eating in the White House Mess. Meeting the commander in chief was not part of the plan, but the boys were excited and hoped they might get such a chance.

Douglas told Michael, "I'm just gonna say, 'Hiya, Pres...'"

On his way out to the lawn to board Marine One, the president came over to say a quick hello. Michael remembers that he had the softest hands of any man he ever met. Douglas just stared, mouth agape.

On the phone the morning of the twenty-third, not yet able to grasp the full enormity of Dallas, Douglas said, "Dad, I'm glad I met him before he got killed."

★ ★ ★

I had no stomach for breakfast.

The Saturday mail came on schedule, mostly routine congressional comments and requests, all but one written before Dallas. That one got my attention, a message possibly hand-delivered, from the Honorable Charles H. Wilson, a Democrat from California's thirty-first district. I read it. I read it again. His Congressional letterhead. His signature. Still unbelieving, I tossed it onto the sofa.

Soon after, the operator put through a call from a guard on the gate, perhaps the same guard who had admitted Bob Aylmer in happier days. "Mr. Daly, Jimmy Breslin is out here. Claims he's not just a reporter, he's your pal. He won't go away. Want me to run him off?"

"No. Send him up."

The timing couldn't have been better. My friend Jimmy was a wonderful grasping, ever climbing hustler, a newsman of the old blue-collar variety seldom found these days. Jimmy always wanted something but had real class and gentleness hidden within his hard shell.

Jimmy plunked his fat ass onto my sofa, lit a cigar, and said, "Well, today the whole freaking world feels as awful as you do."

"Bullshit. Look at this letter. You can't report it but take a look."

I handed him the Congressman's letter. "It had to have been written before the president's blood had coagulated."

"Jesus. Now I've seen it all. What a rat."

"He crawls."

I walked Jimmy back out to the gate, averting my eyes from the mourners and gawkers across the street.

Back in the East Room, the box was still there.

I told the operator I was heading home, got in my Chevy in my space on East End Avenue, and drove out past another silent crowd standing outside the rear fence.

At home, I hugged the boys, sent them out to play in the drizzle, and slumped onto our sofa with Mary in front of the fire. I nibbled at the sandwich she had made for me. It rained harder. I walked through the neighbor's yard, down to a slender neighborhood beach on Lake Barcroft to get the boys out of the cold rain. Michael was just standing there. Douglas had been skipping stones. He turned and gave my leg a hug. The three of us went up to the fire that was giving more smoke than warmth but was easier to watch than television.

The boys asked if this meant Jackie and her children had to move out of the White House. Michael asked what *we* were going to do. I didn't know and didn't know how to tell him that I didn't know.

We kissed them an early goodnight and sent them upstairs. Later I could hear they were still up. Mary and I talked through the night, not saying anything, just talking. Toward the morning, we slept for a couple of hours, then I called for a car. For the first time since arriving in Washington, I dreaded going to work.

★ ★ ★

I checked and ignored a long list of new phone calls and then wandered down to the press office. Pierre Salinger was back. He handed me a copy of the *Herald Tribune*.

"I don't want to know where your pal got that letter."

From Jimmy's column:

> On Saturday—oh, it must have been almost an entire twenty-four hours since the murder of the President of the United States—a member of Congress who represents one of the great centers of culture and human decency from which California is so famous, sat at his desk on Capitol Hill and dictated a letter to Lyndon Baines Johnson.
>
> The letter was received at the White House and was on view there yesterday. The salutation stressed the fact that Lyndon Johnson

was now president. It was addressed to "President Lyndon Johnson, President of the United States."

"Dear Mr. President," it started and read:

"This is to say that I, and it is hoped, all members of Congress, feel it is my duty to stand behind you and support you at this time. I also would like to say at this time that in the 1960 Democratic National Convention at Los Angeles I voted for you against John F. Kennedy."[18]

I tried to call Jimmy at his home in Queens. He had his wife, Rosemary, take the call and claim he was in the shower. I hung up and asked the White House operator to get him on the line. She did. I chewed his fat ass over betraying a confidence and pointed out that he didn't even have the text verbatim.

"Screw you, Daly, maybe I got a couple of words wrong, but the message is right, and you should be glad I sank the bum. Now he's as dead as Kennedy."

"You treacherous bastard." I slammed the phone down, privately delighted.

A new schedule had been delivered to my desk:

Today, Sunday, the 24th of November:

Coffin moved to the Capitol for public viewing.

In that photo on the Capitol steps, with the staff at attention on either side, we're all looking at Jackie and her children on the

---

18 Dean R. Owen, *November 22, 1963: Reflections on the Life, Assassination, and Legacy of John F. Kennedy*.

steps. All of us except Kenny. It's clear from the back of his head that he's watching the coffin containing the president being carried up the stairs. It's no exaggeration to say that box contained Kenny's whole world.

Monday the twenty-fifth, President Johnson called for a national day of mourning.

After the funeral at St. Matthew's, we moved outside. All the cars for diplomatic corps were in place with the world's heads of state in two parallel lines of black vehicles. The cabinet and staff were ready to move behind the line of foreign leaders. The coffin was loaded. The family followed, then the line of dignitaries, presidents, and kings began to move out. At that moment, Jack McNally, who worked in the Executive Office building and had first delivered the news from Dallas to the White House Mess, stepped in front of the procession and motioned our column, the staff, to line up directly behind the first family and ahead of the world leaders, thus slowly leading the way to the Arlington gravesite.

THE EYES OF TEXAS

1963–1964

"...We had little appetite for working under any President other than John Kennedy."

—KENNETH P. O'DONNELL

On December 23, a month and a day after the president's murder, I wrote:

> I used to watch the clock and worry about how little time was left—now I look, and time drags—can it only be an hour, a day, a week since...?

> How can it be? How can I walk by that office, take my sons in to that darkened room...? that truly darkened room...Only a red rug and a very empty chair.

I kept a journal on a few hundred four-by-six index cards that began as notes for a possible book. They became an account of the aftermath of the assassination and my time working for President Johnson. Eventually, the cards devolved into a catalogue of LBJ's flaws. These notes resurfaced in 2017, while my second wife, Christine, was clearing out our basement, about the same time I started work on this book. I thought I had thrown the cards away.

There had been a time when I thought about taking my cards to the press, but then during the Vietnam War, when I was long gone from the West Wing, I decided not to do anything with them. I had imagined the parents of a young Marine killed in Vietnam having to read the ugly things I observed about the man who sent their son to die. A man who took meetings seated on the toilet, made poop jokes, frequently used the N-word, and talked about his balls and his "bunghole."

When I told Christine and our two sons, Charlie and Kevin, why I had deliberately forgotten about the journal, they were horrified. Kevin said that's exactly why I should have *kept* the diary and maybe published it. Those Gold Star parents had a right to know their son's commander in chief as I had known him—deeply depraved, selfish, dishonest, and egomaniacal.

Rediscovering these notes was a lucky break. They were indispensable in writing this chapter. As with so much else of this memoir project, I have Christine to thank for finding them.

★ ★ ★

At a swearing-in for one of Johnson's new people, former Marine Commandant Shoup said to me what we were all thinking, "Chuck, the president really asked me to stay on. I have faith. However, for the first time, I think the Maker has gotten things a little bit fucked up."

In a five-hour meeting called by President Johnson, on November 26, just four days after the assassination, to discuss immediate next steps with Kennedy's staff, he asked, "Where is Ken O'Donnell?"

Larry replied with thinly concealed sarcasm, "He's in a meeting."

Referring to Kenny's significant absence, I said to O'Brien, "That's a tough message, sent so soon."

He just shrugged, "Yeah..."

As vice president, Johnson's relationship with the president was very different from that of his predecessors. The same was true of his transition after inheriting the office. Before FDR got his fatal headache, Truman reportedly had never set foot in the White House. The first thing Truman did was replace Roosevelt's cabinet with his own. Johnson, to his credit, understood the value of continuity following the shock of the assassination. Retaining Kennedy's staff had been the practical political choice and the decent thing to do to make that transition as smooth as possible and to avail himself of the extraordinary team he had so suddenly inherited. Soon after he took over, President Johnson spoke with each of us individually. Then he gathered us to say a few words. These were the same words he had said to me earlier.

"I know you'll never love me the way you loved Jack..."

On the way out of our huddle, I walked down the hall with Kenny and Bobby.

"Kenny, wasn't that a wonderful speech? Did you write it?" I said.

Bobby, who'd had his head down, looked up and said, "Thank you."

The problem I had with Johnson went back to my original sense that he was a deeply flawed man. Unfortunately, the frustrations he had with Kenny may be what caused him to treat his own staff quite differently. On an open line to Bill Moyers, from a White

House car, I overheard him lacing his conversation with one of his gentlest and most loyal supporters with tough talk and criticism totally unlike the syrupy way he talked to the Kennedy holdovers.

On March 16, 1964, *The Saturday Evening Post* ran a story about Johnson's staff being forced to act like clerks or in some cases being demoted to actual clerkdom.

O'Brien recounted a flight with President Johnson, which I recorded on a card:

> "(Johnson) urges O'Brien to 'use your authority, because I'm going to give you more than you had under JFK...Just the unfinished agenda, OK, then, be a millionaire or go bigger in govt or whatever you want...I'll get it for you, just get me by this agenda—by CR, Farm, Pay, poverty and Medicare—even if you have to buy our way by, then I can coast for a few years...I need to coast, I'm tired.'"

The talk turned to Sorensen's spot—O'Brien okays Feldman for General Counsel because LBJ wants him. "We lost two Jews (Schlesinger and Sorensen), so let's promote one."

O'Brien okays because although he dislikes "suck-asses," "we can handle Feldman." Whom he called "field mouse."

Johnson asked O'Brien if he saw the *Saturday Evening Post* article.

"No."

"And how did you like that job, Larry? Up 'til 2:30 a.m., up again at 6:00 a.m. having me chew your tail, Jesus."

He once made a nervous, drunken phone call to Ralph Dungan

to ask about rumors that he and O'Brien were leaving. Johnson said, "If anybody leaves me, I turn the IRS and the FBI on them." Then he turned to Larry O'Brien, who was in the room. "You remember that, Larry. You remember that."

One time I had been instructed to relate to the representatives that Johnson's speech had been well received and that there were thirty-one bursts of applause. When I called to pass this on to the tough-as-nails Adam Clayton Powell Jr., a black congressman from Harlem, he told me, "Chuck, get out, he'll eat you all alive."

Kenny would say of his brief time serving Johnson,

> "It was not that we had any resentment against President Johnson taking his place in the White House, but rather that we had little appetite for working under any president other than John Kennedy."[19]

That's probably how I would have felt if I hadn't been exposed to Johnson's true nature.

As a president, Johnson had done well after inheriting his office in such a dark time, but as a boss he was clumsy, and as a person he was appalling.

I had disliked him from the start because of his war record...or lack thereof. As vice president, and later as president, LBJ frequently wore a little pin in his lapel with vertical red, white, and blue bars: a Silver Star. There was a major problem with that—the circumstances for his being awarded the nation's third highest decoration for bravery in combat were bogus. In 1942, Congressman and Naval Reserve Lieutenant Commander Lyndon Johnson had

---

19   O'Donnell and Powers, *Johnny.*

traveled to the Pacific on a fact-finding mission. He flew aboard a B-26 bomber which was "intercepted by eight hostile fighters," according to the citation which went on to say that Johnson "evidenced marked coolness." That never happened. The bomber encountered mechanical issues before completing its reconnaissance mission and limped home unmolested by the enemy. No member of the crew was decorated for actions that day.[20]

Johnson's medal was a ploy by MacArthur, who had him decorated in exchange for the pledge that he would lobby President Roosevelt for greater resources for MacArthur's forces in the Pacific Theater.

I remember wearing my Silver Star lapel pin to a scheduled meeting with Johnson where I knew that, as always, he'd be wearing his. Johnson lost his train of thought in the meeting. Afterward, Kenny, himself a recipient of the Bronze Star, observed,

"I noticed you were wearing your medal."

Later, Johnson drunkenly bragged to Larry O'Brien that his war record was more impressive than JFK's.

★ ★ ★

Johnson was Kennedy's opposite in his incuriosity and anti-intellectualism. I remember one of my J-school colleagues, Bob Resnick, a remarkably bright but occasionally strange guy, working in the Executive Office Building on some speech writing when the tall Texan caught him staring into space, thinking of closing remarks.

---

20 Julian Borger, "LBJ's Medal for Valor 'Was Sham,'" *The Guardian*, July 6, 2001.

"What are you doing, boy?"

"I'm just thinking, Mr. Vice President."

An hour or so later, Johnson came by Bob's open door again and saw that Resnick had that same vacant look on his face.

"Goddamnit, boy, are you still thinking?"

The Texan's pomposity and machismo were exceeded only by his vulgarity and casual racism. Mary and I got a full dose of both one night at a party at his Forest Hills residence while he was still vice president. We were drinking in the living room with LBJ and a congressman. Lady Bird was upstairs the whole time, apparently wanting no part in the festivities. After a while, she flicked the lights on and off, whereupon the vice president grabbed his crotch over his pants:

"I know when she wants things."

At the end of the evening, Congressman Thornberry, Mary, and I were getting in the vice president's limo to head home.

"I'm gonna go with you," said the vice president, climbing into the vehicle. He turned to the black driver, and asked, "Did you get that bottle of brown?"

"No, Mister Vice President."

"Well, go git it." While the driver went to fetch the bottle, Johnson apologized to us, "Those niggers are forgetful."

In the car, he said, "Now, Mary, I want you and Chuck to go home

and make a baby and call it 'Lyndon,' then I'll give you a heifer."
That did it. When we stopped for a red light at the intersection
of 31st and Wisconsin, Mary and I got out and walked the short
distance home.

In 1964, my Yale classmate, T. George Harris, called me to
fact-check the claim that Johnson used the N-word for a *Look*
magazine article. I confirmed that he had, and they ran the story
without naming me as the source.

Johnson had even used that word speaking directly to a black
man he was looking to bring to the White House.

From my journal, March 23, 1964:

> "Chuck Roche tells me that Louis Martin, the "brightest of the
> administration's negroes (his words.)" But a man R (Roche) says
> is at DNC "because he can't pass the FBI entrance exam" (for the
> White House)."

Roche told me that Johnson had said to Louis Martin, "Louis,
I've got to have another nigger in the White House to replace
Hatcher (an assistant to Pierre Salinger in the Press Office)." He
had referred to an early civil rights bill that he helped pass as
the "nigger bill."

★ ★ ★

As dispirited as I had become, I still had a job to do.

In 1963, JFK had said of the civil rights bill, "If we don't get it this
year, we'll get it next year." He was looking forward to running
against Barry Goldwater as the Republican nominee for presi-

dent, which would all but guarantee a second term along with substantial Democratic gains in the House and Senate.

We knew that support for such a bill had to be bipartisan. We focused on critical Members who could help us get it out of committee and to a vote. We worked to find conservative Republicans who shared the belief that a civil rights bill was vital to the nation. Our congressional liaison team had done much of the groundwork on the civil rights bill while JFK was still alive, but that doesn't diminish the courage it took Johnson to work openly and effectively to lead the final push for the bill and sign it into law knowing that doing so would deal a body blow to the Democratic Party in the South.

On July 2, 1964, I'm standing in a photo of President Johnson signing the civil rights bill in the Oval Office. I'm holding about a dozen fountain pens with which he is signing the bill—dot by dot—and will then give away to the bill's witnesses. I treasure one of the pens, which hangs in a frame in my office along with that photograph and words describing the bill.

★ ★ ★

Just before Kenny left, he gave me a call at a time when he must have known I needed cheering up.

"You remember that revolving door we talked about? Well, your pal Postmaster Gronouski is going to walk into that door tomorrow."

It turns out, Johnson had wanted to unload Gronouski to make room to appoint Larry O'Brien as postmaster general. He summoned Gronouski to his Texas ranch with some special news.

"John, you're from Po-Land. Well, we're gonna make you am-bass-ador to Po-Land."

Gronouski protested. He wanted to stay as postmaster general.

"Son, this is a chance to serve your ancestors, your own people. They're going to be so proud of you. You're going to love Po-Land, and they'll love you in Po-Land."

I called Kenny back as soon as I heard the news.

"Thank you."

"My pleasure."

In the spring of '64, Johnson expressed worry about the forth-coming book being written by O'Brien and O'Donnell: "I can see the headline now, 'Irish Mafia Leaving After Election, Book Indicates Exodus.'" On May 14, I wrote on a card,

> "Johnson knows he is going to lose Kenny. Gave more of the humble routine, praising everyone for the first six months. He had a picture taken with Kenny on one side and O'Brien on the other. 'This should help sell your book,' he said."

Kenny would tell me that the happiest day of his life was when he went to work for John F. Kennedy at the White House, and the second happiest was the day he walked away from that building. Hard old Kenny put these words in my copy of the book he and Dave Powers did end up writing:

> To the only protestant Irishman I ever knew, except in the North... In memory of many good years.

With love,

—Ken

That was extraordinary for him to write "love." I bet he hadn't said that word three times in his life.

To keep me happy, Johnson arranged for Michael and Douglas to fly to California on Air Force One to see their old friends, a gesture of gratitude and political instinct, which he soured with typical crassness:

> "Chuck, your boys' little friends will be waiting on the runway. When they see that big plane with 'U-nited States of America' written on the side, they are going to piss right in their little pants."

I was excited for the boys, but I wanted them to realize that the life ahead of us wasn't going to include trips on Air Force One, so I booked their return on a series of Greyhound buses from California to New York City. On arrival, Douglas was missing most of the hair on one side of his head. Michael explained that his brother had slept on the floor of a bus somewhere west of Chicago, and his hair got stuck to a wad of gum and had to be cut loose.

★ ★ ★

In the midst of figuring out where I would go next, I got an unexpected visit from Edward H. Levi, provost of the University of Chicago, one of those "intellectual cocksuckers" I'd been assigned to as a new hire in the West Wing a lifetime ago. We talked about Mayor Daley, the university, and Chicago politics. I wasn't sure what he wanted from me or where our chat was going.

Levi looked around my office, admiring the windows and the leather sofa.

"It must be hard to leave this job."

"You have got to be kidding me."

He offered me a position as vice president of the university.

The only thing left to do was make a semigracious exit from Johnson's White House. After I had already taken the job in Chicago, I told President Johnson that I was leaving to help my friend, Kennedy's former press secretary, Pierre Salinger, in his run to hold on to the Senate seat to which he'd been appointed following the death of Senator Clair Engle. The day Salinger left to take up his short-term appointment, he called me so say, "At last, I'm out of this fucking building."

BOBBY

1964–1968

"My brother need not be idealized, or enlarged in death beyond what he was in life; to be remembered simply as a good and decent man, who saw wrong and tried to right it, saw suffering and tried to heal it, saw war and tried to stop it."

—SENATOR EDWARD M. KENNEDY

My first move in Chicago was to kiss Mayor Daley's ring. When I went to see him, he told me, "You're going to be a success."

Coming from him, those words felt like a prophecy. Such was his admiration for Kennedy that anyone close to the late president's circle was a made man in Chicago.

Even though Kennedy would have won the election without Illinois, Daley's support throughout the nominating process and campaign had been crucial. The mayor's devotion to the slain president was touching. He would always refer to him as "John Fitzgerald Kennedy" or "the president" even after that title had been passed to Johnson. At some point in my time with Johnson, I had called on Mayor Daley for help on a bill.

He had said, "I can do it for the president, but not for the new guy."

At the end of our first meeting, the mayor asked why I spell Daly without an "E." Unthinking, I responded, "That's the Irish way."

Silence. I was fortunate to survive that blunder.

At the University of Chicago as with the Marine Corps, the West Wing, and the molasses business, I showed up and got to work not knowing my ass from third base. I made friends with the writers Norman Maclean and Saul Bellow. Bellow had been a great admirer of Kennedy. He attended the inaugural gala. In *Humboldt's Gift*, he lamented what Kennedy's death meant for the arts in America. I was amused that the novel also features a character named "Ulick," the protagonist's brother, described thusly,

> "He's been involved in a hundred scandals and lawsuits. He fired shots ten years ago at a car that used his driveway to turn around."[21]

For all of Saul's inner turmoil and self-loathing portrayed in his characters, nothing could compare to the genuine article, the author himself. I remember how he used to talk about his wives. I would ask about his latest ex.

"She swims around me like a shark, pausing only to bite off another pound of flesh."

The University of Chicago had been stigmatized by McCarthyism as a hotbed of left-wing politics. Ed Levi later told me that taking on someone from Kennedy's office with my background might make the university more open to the outside, more connected to national establishments, and therefore less vulnerable to attack. To help with that mission, I hired an old friend, Michael Claffey.

---

21 Saul Bellow, *Humboldt's Gift*.

We had been classmates and friends at Columbia School of Journalism, where we had some unforgettable nights out and lost weekends. Lost weekdays. By the time I got to Chicago, Claffey had to get out of London for some reason. I missed my friend, and I couldn't think of anyone I could trust more, so I brought him to the university as director of development publications.

* * *

I knew that a job in Chicago would deliver me from Johnson and might still give me a base from which to continue working in politics. Fortunately, Levi okayed my trips to California to help Pierre Salinger hold on to his Senate seat, thus upholding my excuse to leave Johnson.

As the fall election loomed, the appointed Senator had to win a popularity contest with voters and the California Democratic establishment. He needed all the help he could get. For one thing, he had alienated Jesse Unruh, the heaviest of Democratic heavies. I could help with that, as I knew the territory from my DSG days and from the West Wing. Salinger also faced the challenge of having to put a campaign together roughly sixty days before the election.

Another critical problem for Pierre was Nancy. He was married to her. That situation seemed hopeless. It was becoming clear that the campaign was a lost cause, but it looked good to have Nancy campaigning with him. My job was to keep them from killing each other long enough to get the photo ops and make the appearances required of a political couple. And by killing each other, I mean literally committing homicide. One morning we were in a small helicopter traveling between events. If this helicopter had stretchers on the skids like the one in Korea, I'd gladly have ridden outside rather than deal with Pierre and Nancy. I took the middle seat between them on the passenger bench hoping to make sure the kids behaved themselves. They were fighting before we even had our seatbelts on. As we were taking off, Pierre reached across my lap and tried to open the door on Nancy's side and push her out. I broke it up, but they both kept screaming. I grabbed her.

> "Nancy, wait a minute. I hear you like to throw pots...You won't have a pot to piss in much less throw if he loses this election. This man is incapable of earning a living any other way. So why don't you shut your fucking mouth, and why don't we all pretend we're friends here."

We started laughing. The pilot was going nuts.

While I was helping Salinger in California, I added Michael Claffey to the campaign payroll. There was no one else I could think of better suited to manage the unmanageable senator.

"What do I do, boss?"

"Simple. Spend every night from now 'til election with the good senator."

"That's it?"

"That's it. Just make sure you're the only one who spends the night with the senator."

Then I told Pierre to tie a knot in his cock and get used to Claffey being with him from now on.

Talking to RFK.

When I flew to Los Angeles, in the first week of June 1968, I was full of hope. Bobby had made us all hopeful again. Mary had been working for his campaign in Indiana districts that seemed likely to go for the racist George Wallace and his running mate, my old pal, General Curtis "Bombs Away" LeMay, while I made trips to California to help Salinger's doomed special election. By June, Pierre was working on Bobby's campaign after having lost his own race. He invited us out for what we hoped would be a victory party following the California primary. We checked into the Ambassador Hotel. We wandered around the sprawl of a hotel, napped a while in the room, and watched the early projections, which looked encouraging. When the polls closed, I called Bobby's room.

"It looks like you're a winner. Why not give the Mayor (Daley) a call? It's getting late in Chicago. Tell him and tell Rostenkowski that California is Hubert's end of the line. Kenny's at the Mayflower (in DC). I'll give him a call."

"It's very close. What if I don't win?"

"Without California, you're dead anyway. So why not make the call?"

"Okay. See you later."

Mary and I went downstairs to wait outside the crowded ballroom where Bobby addressed the crowd. Maybe he decided not to place the call because he didn't have time. Maybe he was unsure. Maybe he wanted Kenny to first push Rostenkowski for support. Maybe he wanted to call the mayor himself in the morning. How many maybes that night? Maybe if not through the kitchen.

He closed his speech with a rallying cry, "So, my thanks to all of you and on to Chicago and let's win there."

As planned, Bobby ducked the crowd by exiting through the kitchen. The night split open with the unmistakable *pop pop pop* of a small caliber weapon. I ran toward the shots.

Paul Schrade, Bobby's pal from the United Auto Workers, was on the floor, bleeding from a head wound, eyes open and looking dead. Just beyond, Bobby was on his back with a crowd surging around him. Some of us tried to make a protective ring to give him air. I grabbed a hand with my right, and felt a sharp, familiar pain in my left arm when someone pulled on it to complete the human barrier. It was Jesse Unruh. He was yelling at some others who were holding a thrashing little figure, the gunman: "Don't kill him."

I shouted to Fred Dutton, who was inside the barrier with Bobby, "Somebody loosen his tie."

Bobby was lying on his back, motionless, his mouth slightly open. There was almost no blood except on the back of one hand. No visible entry or exit wounds. His eyes had that stare I'd seen before but never from anyone who survived. I saw Jim Ables. I saw Rocky.

Rocky had mumbled, "Corpsman."

Ables had said, "Oh shit."

Bobby was silent.

★ ★ ★

In DC, earlier that night, Kenny O'Donnell and Paul Kirk, a key man in Bobby's campaign who, like O'Donnell, had been Bobby's football teammate at Harvard, had eaten dinner with Rostenkowski at Paul Young's, working to persuade him to back Bobby instead of the party's initial choice, Hubert Humphrey. After dinner, O'Donnell and Kirk retired to a room at the Mayflower Hotel, where they watched the early returns come in from California and went to bed.

I called, assuming they had already heard about Bobby. An unfamiliar voice answered.

"This is Chuck Daly, who's this?"

"Paul Kirk."

"You guys aren't watching TV?"

"No. It's late here."

"Put Kenny on."

"Kenny, Bobby's been shot. In the head."

"I'll see you at the funeral," he said and hung up.

Kenny left Paul in the room and returned after sunrise. Though Paul doesn't know for sure, he believes Kenny spent the night at the president's grave in Arlington.

★ ★ ★

I remember hoping for a miracle, but I knew head wounds and miracles don't mix.

Pierre had raced to the hospital, riding on the back of a policeman's motorcycle. When I arrived, he told me to handle the phones. Among the calls, I answered one from Jimmy Breslin, "Once one of those .38 bullets starts rattling around in your head, you're gone."

I told him it sounded more like a pop gun. I was right. The runt had fired a .22, one of the tiniest bullets there is, more commonly used for shooting tin cans and squirrels. One bullet had gone in the soft spot behind Bobby's ear, sending fragments of bullet and bone into his brain.

I called Mayor Daley with the bad news.

He said, "Those police out there are no good."

As if Chicago cops were any better.

Twenty-six hours after the shooting, Robert F. Kennedy was pronounced dead at 1:44 a.m., June 6, 1968. He was forty-two years old.

* * *

On the flight to New York, a stewardess wept with Mary.

The funeral at St. Patrick's was packed.

Jackie had asked Leonard Bernstein to arrange the music. Andy Williams's unaccompanied voice belted out a rendition of "The Battle Hymn of the Republic."

Ted read Bobby's own words from the pulpit, challenging us to carry on his unfinished work:

> "It is from numberless diverse acts of courage and belief that human history is shaped. Each time a man stands up for an ideal, or acts to improve the lot of others, or strikes out against injustice, he sends forth a tiny ripple of hope, and crossing each other from a million different centers of energy and daring, those ripples build a current that can sweep down the mightiest walls of oppression and resistance."

It was hot on the funeral train. We ran out of ice somewhere in New Jersey, on the way to the Capitol by way of Delaware and Maryland, so we drank our whiskies neat. Arthur Schlesinger Jr. described the journey as a "wake on wheels." The mood is better captured by Frank Mankiewicz, Bobby's press secretary,

> "An interesting cultural thing was happening on the train...the Irish were having a wake, the protestants were at a funeral, and the Jews were weeping and carrying on—they'd have torn their clothes off if they'd thought of it—looking out the window and empathizing with the people outside, weeping for the full eight or nine hours. The protestants sort of sat stiffly and consoled each other. The Irish drank."[22]

We moved through backyards, dirty embankments, discarded railroad ties and bottles and trash, and a corridor of humanity beside the tracks and on porches, balconies, and rooftops. They made signs of prayer, they saluted, they waved.

The economist John Kenneth Galbraith observed,

> "If you were burying Ronald Reagan you would obviously want to do it with an airplane; but if you're going to bury Robert Kennedy, his people live along the railway tracks."[23]

In a New Jersey suburb, Kenny and I had looked over the crowd and noticed a foursome of golfers on a distant hill.

"Kenny, look at those bastards not even missing a putt."

---

22   Jean Stein, *American Journey: The Times of Robert Kennedy*, 61.

23   *American Journey.*

"Don't worry about that. This is New Jersey, whether they know it or not, they all voted for Kennedy."

In the last car, with the family, friends, and the coffin, I heard Ethel say to her son, "Wave back, Joe."

FORTUNATE SON

1963–1988

"It ain't me, it ain't me, I ain't no senator's son."

—CREEDENCE CLEARWATER REVIVAL, "FORTUNATE SON"

Back in 1963, in his efforts to build support for overdue legislation on civil rights, Bobby Kennedy, then attorney general, was getting more heat than help from the American Bar Association and the legal profession as a whole. He asked me if I knew any Republican lawyers who might be willing to stand up. I said I knew one, a busted-out Marine hero who lived out in the sticks in the Portola Valley, a rural paradise behind Stanford's 8,180 acres.

After Korea, Pete McCloskey had gone back to law school. In 1963, I called Pete and invited him to a special White House conference on civil rights. Pete left that meeting eager to have a new opportunity to serve. As a lawyer, Pete would join with our friend, Lew Butler, a veteran of the Peace Corps, in taking on un-Republican causes like equal housing. In 1967, Pete ran for Congress against the former child actress, Shirley Temple, in the Republican primary for the special election following the death of Arthur J. Younger. By then, the Vietnam War was on and Pete promised to be the first Republican congressman to oppose the war. Between this unpopular stance and his opponent's celebrity, we all assumed his was a lost cause. To everyone's surprise but his own, Pete won his election, a victory that became known as "the sinking of the Good Ship Lollipop."

★ ★ ★

Pete took a hands-on approach to opposing the Vietnam War that involved going there to see it for himself. He put together a privately funded trip with money raised by our friend, Mike Brewer, a bright young Republican of Pete's "party of Abe Lincoln" who had managed to establish a dialogue between student antiwar groups and more conservative elements. I told Pete I had a strong hunch there'd be an "accident" over there. A jeep would roll over, a chopper would go down, something taking the peacenik Republican from California permanently out of the debate.

"So, I'm coming with you."

This trip to our second war together became a book, *Truth and Untruth*, which I helped Pete get published through my agent, Sterling Lord. Pete had suspected the war was bullshit from the get-go. This was confirmed when Daniel Ellsberg, a Marine who worked at the Pentagon, gave Pete an advanced look at the top-secret Pentagon Papers that he had smuggled out of the Pentagon a few pages at a time and would eventually make public. Pete had gone to Vietnam in 1968, between Christmas and his swearing in as a congressman. I tagged along on his second trip, in '71. By then, antiwar sentiment had grown, following Nixon's bombing and invasion of neutral Cambodia. Yet the Republican party line was still pro-war. Pete had been booed on the House floor and it looked as though he might be ousted from the party.

★ ★ ★

The fundraising for the trip to Vietnam is described in Jimmy Breslin's *How the Good Guys Finally Won: Notes from an Impeachment Summer*. We brought along John Dominis, a *Life* photographer who had covered Korea and had taken the famous "black power salute" photo at the 1968 Olympics in Mexico City; Congressman Jerry Waldie; the reporter Lou Cannon; and Paul Lafond, a Marine lieutenant colonel who was hospitalized for psychiatric reasons after leading a battalion in Vietnam. I hoped, for our sake, that there would be strength in numbers and that we wouldn't all get greased at once. Our group was presented with an official itinerary by our military minders. Pete pocketed that plan and came up with his own as we went along.

In one village, an American general spoke triumphantly about moving civilians around from one village to another to make our operations run more smoothly and stay one step ahead of the Viet Cong.

Upon hearing this, Pete saw an opportunity to give the general a history lesson.

"Do you know General Jodl, sir?"

"No, I never served with him."

"No no, you wouldn't have. He was a Nazi. We hanged him at Nuremberg for doing exactly what you're talking about here."

Having strong words with Pete in Vietnam. We settled this argument by running a race on the runway behind us.

Wandering around one of our bases, I went into a big tent set up as a crude bar. The place was full of Marines drinking. I started chatting with a pilot. I introduced myself as a busted-out platoon leader traveling with a fellow Korean war vet and trying to see what's going on over here.

He shouted to no one in particular, "Hey, watch out, this is one of those guys they warned us about."

"Well, fuck you."

"No, hey, relax, pal. You want to know what I do?" He said, "I fly the ARVN (Army of the Republic of Vietnam—our allies) officers home overnight and fly them back in the morning."

"You leave the enlisted guys?"

I tried to imagine a world in which Pete and I got to chopper off the battlefield every night with the other gentlemen officers, leaving the enlisted swine to fend for themselves and hope they're still there when we punch in again in the morning. What. The. Fuck?

"That's right. Anyone who thinks we can win this war is out of his fucking mind," said the Marine.

★ ★ ★

Back in the States, Pete ran for president against Nixon on an antiwar platform and took 11 percent of the vote in the New Hampshire primary and a single vote at the Republican National Convention.

After Watergate, Pete would be the first Republican to call for Nixon's impeachment. He was cofounder of Earth Day and was instrumental in cleaning up California's air and water. In 1982, he ran for the Senate, where he would have had a stronger national voice. Unfortunately, he committed political suicide by advocating for fair treatment of the Palestinians in their conflict with Israel.

★ ★ ★

Of all the battles Pete and I fought together over the years, none was more personally satisfying or a more clear case of good vs. evil than the time we took on a TV preacher pretending to be a Marine combat veteran.

In 1986, the Reverend Pat Robertson announced his candidacy for president. Using his TV pulpit, he raised ten times as much as the other major candidates—George H.W. Bush and Bob Dole. To a certain kind of American conservative, Robertson looked very appealing: he was a man of letters, with a degree from Yale, and a man of God who promised to set our great nation on the path of Christian values. On top of all that, Pat claimed to be a "combat Marine" with experience fighting the Communists in the hills of Korea. There were two problems with his claim, however. First, Marines who've been in combat seldom call ourselves "combat Marines." But there was another, much bigger problem with Robertson's story. It was false.

When I first heard him brag about combat experience, I thought to myself: *That's interesting, but I seem to remember him getting off the troop ship in Japan.*

While Pat was steaming west across the Pacific along with Pete and Jim Ables, me, and the other lieutenants of the fifth replacement draft, Pat's daddy, who was a senator from Virginia, was working to keep his son out of combat. Pat had asked him to do this.

Senator Robertson was using his influence, with the Commandant of the Marine Corps, to get his son reassigned to Japan. The pretense was that Pat needed "additional training"—as if the rest of us didn't need some of that. Higher up, it was arranged that five other lieutenants were pulled from the ship as beards to conceal the reason for Pat's reassignment. This meant that six platoons either didn't get their replacement lieutenant, or some man whose turn it was didn't get to go home. It's unclear if anyone paid the ultimate price for Pat Robertson's cowardice.

Representative McCloskey and Robertson had first clashed when the Reverend accused our fellow Korean War veteran, Andy Jacobs, a congressman from Indiana running for reelection, of being "soft on communism." When Robertson bragged about his alleged combat experience in his presidential campaign, Pete and a couple other Marines, who remember him getting off the ship, went to the press with the truth. The story got attention as Robertson's candidacy gained popularity and viability. By that point, Robertson had already filed a libel suit against Pete seeking $35 million in damages. Though the legal battle promised to be inconvenient and financially devastating, Pete welcomed it, believing that the facts would come out in open court. Over the sixteen months that followed the October 1986 lawsuit, Pete would spend $400,000 to research the incident. Luckily, Pete's homeowner's liability insurance covered almost all his costs.

Pete's digging unearthed damning evidence that Robertson was lying. Letters from Robertson, sent from aboard the ship, thanked his dad for calling in the favor and proved not only that he benefited from special treatment but that he had asked for it.

In sworn testimony, a bunkmate of Robertson's at Quantico stated that upon learning that his name was on the list of those assigned to lead rifle companies, Robertson told him that he intended to call his "Daddy" to get him out of it.

Another Marine stated, "My memory is that he said words to that effect, that, 'I called my Daddy and I'm going to try to have him get me off,' or 'I will see if I can get stationed in Japan,' or something of that sort."

The officer who assigned Pat to Japan testified that his father's political influence had in fact been the reason. Eventually, two of the beards who had been pulled from the ship complained to a visiting general. They knew that the situation was rotten and wanted to accept their duty to go to war. They got their wish. Both were wounded. Robertson was also sent to Korea, but he was assigned to the safety of headquarters. Up until that point, he had been stationed on a base in Japan, where his job was going back and forth to Korea to keep the officer's club in the rear well stocked with booze. For this, he was affectionately nicknamed "the Liquor Officer," a moniker that was widely reprinted in newspapers across the country during the Republican primary. Incredibly, that was the revelation that really bothered Robertson and some of his people.

Lying about service was one thing, slandering men who did fight was another, but to be associated with liquor as one who claims to speak directly to God...But Robertson had not yet been born again in Korea. He was, as one buddy of his remembers, "No evangelist at that time, just a typical young Marine."

In their effort to disprove the "liquor officer claim," his defense team would end up putting all sorts of "typical Marine" behavior—and some behavior that's out of bounds even for the saltiest among us—in the public record.

After a Marine named Brosman testified that Robertson had in fact made liquor errands, Robertson's attorney tried to discredit the man by asking whether in fact he had any direct contact with Robertson.

Q: Do you recall any specific conversations you might have had with Pat Robertson?

A: Well, yeah. He was scared to death he had gonorrhea and was very relieved when he found out it was what the corpsmen called "nonspecific drip."

Q: Well, isn't it true that this "nonspecific drip" is not the kind of disease transmitted by sexual intercourse or anything else, that it's an infection of the urinary tract?

A: Right. But he thought he had gonorrhea. And I don't think he got that from any other source.

Q: How do you recall Pat Robertson being in those days?

A: Well, I—it's hard to say...he was more inconsiderate, pretty inconsiderate for, I mean, things like the cleaning girl.

We had a cleaning girl who came in. It's like the story of the fraternity house and the nineteen-year-old housemother. We had a cleaning girl who was nineteen who was our maid in our barracks. But she was a nice Korean girl.

And we had a lot of prostitutes around there, for example. And, well, Pat used to fool around with her all the time. That is, pinching her and carrying on.

And every once in a while, he would chase her outside the house and then he would continue chasing her and pinching her outside the house.

That would terrify her because the Koreans would see.

And, of course, these prostitutes were dead meat when we left because they had ruined their lives to make money off of the Americans.

But once the Americans left, they were really finished.

And she didn't want the Korean men to see her fooling around like with an American. And she'd plead with him to stop and he wouldn't stop. And none of the rest of us would have done that.[24]

The lawyer's next question really bothers me because he seems to imply that we all got up to a bit of sexual assault over there.

Q: You never saw anyone else messing around with women?

A: Oh, not none of the—not with that maid.

Oh, a lot of guys messed around with the prostitutes that wanted to get messed around with, including Pat.[25]

Ugly stuff but devastating. The timing couldn't have been better, or worse for Pat. The trial was set to begin on March 8, 1988, "Super Tuesday." The week before the election, after watching some of the coverage of the whole mess on TV, a former corpo-

---

24 Paul N. McCloskey, *The Taking of Hill 610*.

25 *The Taking of Hill 610*.

ral, Leo T. Cronin, wrote to the *Marin County Coastal Pilot* of his memories of Robertson, whom he remembers as "clean shaven and showered."

Cronin, like Robertson, was a headquarters Marine, but he's humble and honest about it, "The line company Marines I saw smelled badly, looked poorly...Neither Robertson nor I could carry their gear."

He remembers seeing truckloads of frozen bodies of line Marines driving past his safe position in the rear. He said Robertson was now "trying to get elected by standing on those frozen bodies I saw..."[26]

The letter appeared on the front page and was widely circulated.

The Liquor Officer didn't carry a single state on "Super Tuesday" and would formally drop out in May.

Sometimes, I get frustrated looking back on this episode. I wish more could have been done to expose Robertson's lies to his viewership of generally honest and good people who believe they're doing right by their Higher Power to send Pat $700 a year, thus earning membership in the "700 Club" for which his TV show is named. I wish our system wasn't so vulnerable to conmen and smug liars like him.

But then I tell myself at least Robertson got some of what he deserved. *Drip by drip.*

---

26 "Pat Robertson 'No Combat Marine,'" *Marin County's News Weekly,* February 7, 1988, 15-21.

HOPE AND HISTORY

1975–2015

"Bloodshed for political change prevents the only change that truly matters: in the human heart."

—JOHN HUME, NOBEL LECTURE

When my youngest son, Kevin, was considering joining the Marine Corps, he asked my friend, General Michael Lehnert, for advice. Mike told Kevin, "The Corps will teach you how to kill, but they cannot teach you how to get over killing."

I stayed out of that conversation because I didn't want to influence Kevin's decision one way or another, but I wouldn't want my son or anyone's son to go to war without some idea of what it's really like.

By sharing my story, I hope I communicate a sense of what it's like to go to war and what it's like to live with the undying memories. In these pages, you can see the disproportionate impact of less than six months of combat in a long, full life. Writing a memoir, I became the editor of my own life story. Some of what I left out includes the riots in Chicago, my time as Harvard's vice president and my work at the Joyce Foundation in Chicago, where I helped grow a modest fund to a billion dollar organization that makes grants of roughly $30 million a year on issues like schools, water quality, civil rights, gun violence, and the arts.

Those chapters of my life were interesting, to put it mildly. I'm as proud of my service on various boards as I am of anything else I've done, but when it comes to telling my life story in a way that might help and inspire others, I've chosen to focus on the war and my time in public service. I have a feeling that someone eager to run Harvard or sit on an influential board doesn't need my story to motivate them, but I just might be able to help someone who's coming out of Walter Reed, maimed inside and out and wondering what he or she can make of themselves with 40 percent disability and a head full of painful memories and damaged hopes.

★ ★ ★

In 1975, I became involved with the beginnings of The American Ireland Fund, a role that brought me back to Ireland and back to war. By that point, the situation in Northern Ireland had gone from terrible to seemingly hopeless.[27]

At the time I became involved with the conflict in the North, many Americans wanted to help the Republican cause, but unfortunately that "help" often took the form of money for guns. Those interested in promoting peace had few options and no way to ensure that their dollars weren't being funneled toward gunmen. I recall one conversation I had with a Chicago politician who sup-

---

27 A little background: In 1922, the thirty-six counties that make up The Republic of Ireland gained independence from Great Britain. Six counties in the north of Ireland remained part of the United Kingdom, which they still are as of this writing. Catholics in the North were denied basic civil rights, housing, and employment opportunities. By the late 1960s, what started as a civil rights movement had devolved into urban warfare between the mostly Catholic Republicans who wanted the North to join the Republic of Ireland, and the mostly protestant loyalists who wanted it to remain part of the UK and were supported by the police and British army. This conflict, which continued until the 1998 Good Friday Agreement, is known as "The Troubles."

ported a front for the Irish Republican Army (IRA). She believed her money would fund hospital beds.

"No. That money is for putting people *in* hospital beds," I told her.

I knew there had to be others who felt the way I did. One person vitally interested in helping was Tony O'Reilly, the Babe Ruth of Irish rugby who had gone on to business success in international newspapers and as chairman of Heinz. Tony partnered with his friend, Dan Rooney, the Irish American owner of the Pittsburgh Steelers, to establish The American Ireland Fund. The pair were legends of sport, but despite their impressive backgrounds, their lack of military experience could have been exploited by those hostile fakers in the North who presented themselves as peacemakers and freedom fighters. Someone pointed out that I'd be a good member of the Fund's new board: an ex-warrior who opposed violence in Ireland and elsewhere.

"The most violent nonviolent person you can imagine," is how someone described me to them.

I didn't know what could be done about Ireland. All I knew was how I felt about the realities of violence. I was against killing because I knew a thing or two about killing. I knew there wasn't any glory in it. I knew dying was never as clean or simple as patriotic legends of martyrdom make it seem.

It's easy to say you want peace. But to put in the work to make peace happen, that's another matter. It takes courage in a place where peace means putting violent men out of business, in a place where you don't have any easy answers for people who are still angry once the shooting stops. During the peace talks in the 1990s, one man underscored that point.

"I'm told I must shake the hand of the man who killed my son and say I forgive him."

That's exactly what was needed. It was not easy. I couldn't have done it.

For the Ireland Fund, raising money for peace and culture was a matter of tiptoeing through a minefield of fronts and unscrupulous characters on both sides who needed money to carry on their war and were full of tricky ways to get it. If our promise was to provide a way for Americans to send money to Ireland for peace, we would be finished if a single penny ended up in a gunman's pocket. We had to follow up with our grantees to make sure they were legit. I went to Belfast and Derry to check on our most sensitive grants in person and endorse their work.

Northern Ireland is a small place where trust is a currency that's not squandered on outsiders. I was greeted with suspicion everywhere. The Republicans only needed to know my first name to know I was a "prod" (protestants are named after kings; Catholics, saints). The Brits thought any American hanging out in their domestic war zone had to be a Paddy/Yank gunrunner. An act of government, not unlike America's Patriot Act, gave the British the power to detain such persons without cause. My fellow protestants might wonder what I was doing talking to the "papists." And anyone who, like myself, dreamed of a Northern Ireland without bombs, roadblocks, and barbed wire, may have doubted my motives and sincerity.

Early one morning, walking in a rough Republican area, I was approached by a four-man patrol of British soldiers. They were young and nervous. They demanded my papers. I knew it was better to show them my American passport than my Irish one, in my other pocket. At the very least, it would make it more complicated for them to harm me. The first president of Ireland was spared a British firing squad during the revolution because he had been born in Brooklyn.

"What are you doing here?" one of them asked.

"What are *you* doing here?" I replied.

He put the muzzle of his weapon under my chin and suggested I answer their questions.

* * *

We could babysit our money all we wanted, but it wouldn't do any good if we didn't connect with people in the communities who shared our dreams of peace and our will to take action to help those dreams become reality. Peace isn't the absence of conflict, it's the presence of all the wonderful things that get pushed aside when the fighting starts—peace is art and culture and music. It's desegregated sports teams and schools. It's having better things to do than kill and die over religion and politics.

Jackie Redpath calls all this "the hardcore stuff of daily life." Jackie grew up in the Shankill, an underprivileged protestant neighborhood in West Belfast. In his effort to build an integrated community center, he took enormous personal risk to seek out Catholics who shared his hope for peace. This at a time when even whispers that you were seen talking to someone from the other side could be a death warrant.

Another heroic protestant we worked with was Judy Hayes. Even though she grew up middle class, her life had not been free from the absurd and petty cruelties of the conflict. She came from an area where the only school available was a Church of Ireland (protestant) school that wasn't very good. Her parents negotiated with the Catholic Convent of Mercy: she could attend their school provided she didn't talk to the other children at recess. Judy's work with the Ireland Fund was a credit to both sides and to the hopes for an Ireland without sides. She put together the advisory council made up of Catholics and protestants from throughout the North and the Republic of Ireland, which became our system for vetting grant applications and evaluating results. We would have been lost without that council.

Feeding the donkeys at my summer home in Ireland.

At some point, my charitable work connecting Ireland and Irish America, my service to my adoptive nation, and my work at that school in Cambridge got me considered for an appointment to return to the Emerald Isle as Ambassador of the United States of America. It was between the *New York Times* journalist Bill Shannon and me. House Speaker Tip O'Neill favored me. Senator Ted Kennedy wanted Shannon. It came down to a committee that included a professor, Stanley Hoffman from Harvard. Hoffman informed the Baptist President Jimmy Carter, "Chuck Daly swears all the time."

Shannon got the fucking appointment.

★ ★ ★

I met Christine Sullivan at a party on St. Patrick's Day, 1977, at Congressman Don Edward's apartment at the Watergate where he was hosting a reception honoring Betty Williams and Mairead Corrigan, who'd been jointly awarded the Nobel Peace Prize for their work in Northern Ireland. Christine remembers it as her "first big Washington party." She was working as a powerhouse scheduler for Tip O'Neill, the newly elected Speaker of the House. Christine remembers me as a pushy jerk, because I wanted something from the Speaker and wouldn't take her "no" for an answer. I remember being charmed by her toughness. We met again that weekend at another Irish party. Amid all the bullshit and climbing of Washington after hours, here was this beautiful, patient woman who seemed to be listening to everything I said. Later I learned that she listened so intently because I mumble when I talk, and she couldn't understand a word I was saying, but she liked the way I tended to talk in stories.

Christine was born on February 18, 1951, the same week I landed in Korea. On November 22, 1963, she was a seventh grader at Our Lady of the Presentation Grammar School, in Brighton, Massachusetts. In Washington, she had worked on Title IX and the Equal Rights Amendment. She was the Speaker's ambassador to the many women's groups lobbying on Capitol Hill, working with the Congressional Women's Caucus, the leaders of NOW, Gloria Steinem, Congresswomen Bella Abzug and Pat Schroeder, and others. She had been assigned the staff leader, responsible for the health and safety of women members of Congress on a trip to Thailand and Cambodia, where they were the first Westerners in the country after Pol Pot's genocide.

I was amazed by Christine. I loved Mary and I was falling in love with Christine. It was frustrating and awkward. There was no chance I would leave Mary, and Christine knew that. In some ways that made things more difficult; not only had I gone outside my marriage, but this other woman loved me enough to stay with me in a seemingly hopeless situation.

MARY

1987

"...To the land of rest that is unending
All peacefully from Bantry Bay"

—"BANTRY BAY," IRISH FOLK SONG

Through the 1980s, I was increasingly dividing my time between
the Joyce Foundation and the American Ireland Fund. It was as
close to retired as I was comfortable with. My schedule made it
possible to spend more time in Bantry, West Cork, Ireland, where
Mary and I had built a summer cottage. By then, Michael and
Betsy Claffey had bought a house in Kilchrohane, over a treacherous mountain road from us. We had dinners and long summer
nights looking out on the water.

Then our world changed. Mary found a lump in her breast. Cancer.
She had it treated. It came back. It spread. By 1987, it was clear
that further treatment was hopeless.

We celebrated my sixtieth birthday at our Cape house, where
a local contractor, Scott Sveningson, had ignored local zoning
laws to build a deck for her to watch the sunset from. At the party,
Mary took Betsy Claffey aside and whispered one of her recipes.

Her way of saying goodbye and seeing that I didn't starve after she was gone.

Mary wanted to die in Ireland. We went to Bantry.

I did my best with the cooking and cleaning, but I couldn't carry her because of my arm. My precious neighbors, Sean and Teresa O'Luasa, arranged for a nurse to help. A local doctor made house calls and confirmed what we already knew. No hope.

The nurse who came to the house every day refused to accept payment because of what Mary had done to help some local women in times of difficulty.

The day came when the doctor said, "I can promise you there'll be no more pain."

"Doc, let me tell you something. If there's any more pain, you'll find the two of us in the garage in the car with the engine running."

Mary and I spent our last moments together in bed.

She was thirsty but couldn't swallow. I wet her lips to ease the dryness.

"Can I have a Paddy (whiskey)?"

I went to the kitchen, poured the whiskey, and brought the glasses to the bed, drank some, and bent over to let a few drops dribble from my kiss into her mouth.

June 16, 1987. Early light glinted off the water. Hungry Hill, across the bay, was purple in the calm palette of dawn. Our little inboard cabin cruiser, *Titanic II*, tugged at its mooring.

"You should eat." Teresa O'Luasa, our friend and neighbor came by. "Mary told me, 'Go have lunch with Paddy.'"

At the bar in O'Connor's, my friend Paddy and I had toasted cheese sandwiches and whiskey.

When I got home, Teresa was sitting alone in the living room. That worried me.

In the bedroom, Mary was asleep and breathing very slowly. I lay beside her.

Her breathing got slower and slower.

Her breathing stopped.

I kissed her. I didn't want to leave her.

The doctor came, and the nurse, and the hearse. I pretended that I hadn't seen the bandage the nurse had tied around her head to keep Mary's jaw from dropping open.

Teresa gave me a hug. She told me that our favorite donkey had bitten one of the men carrying Mary away.

Then I was alone. Toward the evening, the tide was out. I went down to the beach. My pistol was an ocean away. Fuck it. I begged God to finish the job, that I was still here was the only thing crueler than her being gone.

I knelt in the wet sand and prayed as hard as I'd ever prayed for Mary's life, one of the few times I've ever prayed: "Please, God, give me cancer."

★ ★ ★

The walls of St. Brendan's are etched and inlaid with praise for various long dead lords and ladies who used to own this piece of Ireland.

When Michael was giving his eulogy, he placed a hand upon his mother's casket, gazed up at those walls and said, "If you want to talk about royalty, here she is."

Ireland's prime minister, Garret FitzGerald, sat in one of the pews. His tribute to her appeared in *The Irish Times,*

> "Mary Daly cared passionately for people...She found violence intolerable...all the more so because for her the real Ireland was epitomized by the warmth and decency of the people of Bantry whom she had come to know and love so well."[28]

At the wake in JJ Crowley's, an old-fashioned pub that hosts wakes and, on Friday nights, Irish music and dancing, our Bantry friends mingled with friends from Chicago, Washington, California, and Dublin.

Unbeknownst to me, Michael Claffey from the University of Chicago and Dick Donahue were talking business at the bar. Dick was on the board of the Kennedy Library, in Boston, and was

---

28 The Ireland Fund, *For the Love of Bantry, The Mary Daly Fund Celebrates 30 Years of Impact For West Cork*, accessed August 29, 2020, https://irelandfunds.org/flipbooks/connect-ss2018/inc/html/35. html?page=34.

looking for a director of the Library Museum and Foundation. He mentioned this to Claffey, who replied, "I don't know why you're looking anywhere else. You've got the guy for the job right here."

The Yanks all flew home, Prime Minister Garret FitzGerald and other august friends returned to their lives, and I was alone in our drafty house on Bantry Bay listening to the breakers on the stone beach. I putt-putted around the bay in the *Titanic II*. I found remote and sheltered places to anchor for the night and slept in the cabin.

At the wake, Dick had asked me, "How many people come to that little protestant church?"

"Not many, maybe a couple dozen; I don't go. But up the hill, the Catholic church fills up every Sunday. Last year, St. Brendan's roof started caving in due to lack of funds for repairs. So, on Sunday, the Catholic church had a second collection to rebuild the protestant roof."

A little while after Dick flew back to Lowell, St. Brendan's priest showed me a letter from him.

> "Here's a check to help fix your roof not for what goes on underneath it."

THE DREAM

1987–2001

"...the work goes on, the cause endures, the hope still lives, and the dream shall never die."

—TED KENNEDY, SPEAKING AT RFK'S FUNERAL

A few months after Mary's funeral, Dick called and asked me what my plan was. He told me that he had a job opening for me if I was interested in doing something besides looking after the donkeys and feeling sorry for myself. He told me it was a federal government job at the John Fitzgerald Kennedy Presidential Library. A nod from an old pal wouldn't suffice, but my service and medals and prior federal employment, including my time in Kennedy's own West Wing, would make me well qualified.

I got the job, flew to Boston and, at age sixty, started a new career.

★ ★ ★

The JFK Presidential Library and Museum was conceived in January 1964, less than sixty days after the President's assassination, when Attorney General Robert Kennedy announced the creation of an oral history project to be developed over the coming years. Kenny, Dick, myself, and 150 others shared our memories in the first rounds of interviews. The number of participants more than doubled through the 1970s. Thus began an archive, warehoused in Waltham, Massachusetts, and curated by a skeleton staff: Dave Powers, Dan Fenn, and Donna Smerlas. At that time, the archive was inaccessible to scholars and the public.

By the end of '64, I.M. Pei had been chosen to design the building that would house the archives and museum. The next step was to find a location. Jackie wanted Cambridge and Harvard. However, this proposal drew protests in a classic "not in my backyard" situation. There were fears of traffic in an already congested part of town, and the prediction of over one million new visitors to the neighborhood annually was seen as a burden rather than a blessing. The fight was still raging when I got to Harvard. By then, LBJ had already seen his own presidential library completed and dedicated in Austin, Texas. I was in favor of the Harvard location; it would have been good for both the library and Harvard. But by 1975, the plan was scrapped.

Meanwhile, the University of Massachusetts's Boston campus, under the leadership of Bob Wood, a former member of the Kennedy administration, had been pitching their own proposal to Jackie, hustling for the university's land to be used to build the library. A committee went with that idea and decided to build it out at Columbia Point among some ugly university buildings, around the corner from a rough housing project and a beach where gangland murder victims were buried, on a windswept appendix of land that had once been an actual dump. They envisioned potential in the site, focusing on the sea and the city skyline.

In 1977, they broke ground out at Columbia Point. Eleven years later, I was running the place.

Dinner with Jackie Kennedy at the JFK Library.

One of my first acts as director was making a small change to I.M. Pei's magnificently designed building and its beautiful landscaped grounds designed by Bunny Mellon to look like a Cape Cod garden. There was a public phone booth out front that was not at all in keeping with the atmosphere or the look of the library. To have it removed would have been a bureaucratic hassle, so I used a saw to render it out of order. Moving forward with this approach, I set about cutting the excess verbiage in our official communications. They had this way of communicating on the federal side of the organization where persons were addressed in writing by the acronyms of their titles and departments. It was a formality that I was no good at and didn't want to be good at. I sent a memo to the staff urging them to write about humans like humans. I said that we'd have to say goodbye to our friends like NPP and NPN, "and that well rested NAPP."

Concerning another nonissue, I got a call from the chief archivist of the United States, who asked me, "What do you plan to do about alcohol at the Kennedy Library?"

"We plan to keep taking it orally, unless you have any other suggestions."

★ ★ ★

The Kennedy Library has been called "the crown jewel of Boston tourism." The beauty of the building, its view of the harbor and the city skyline, draw forums and events. We've hosted heads of state, kings, presidents, great political minds, and the heroic recipients of the annual Profile in Courage award. But of all the events that we hosted during my time at the library, the one I'm proudest of is one that I organized and helped fund for the men of Charlie Company. I made a deal with the caterer, Bob Wiggins Gourmet Caterers—who are used to cooking gourmet meals for the leaders of industry and government. We'd have been happy to reminisce over cold C-rations and fruit cocktails, but the caterers surprised us with a banquet on par with anything they've served at the library for which they charged us twenty-five dollars a head. As at every reunion, we had one table set with a single empty place for our fallen brothers.

★ ★ ★

During my tenure at the library, we built a spectacular function space where we could host forums and special events. I.M. Pei's glass building was beautiful to look at and look out of, but the acoustics were a nightmare. I once had to apologize to the cellist Yo-Yo Ma for the sound quality after he played for one of our dinners.

That gracious man remarked, "That's okay, Chuck, I enjoyed hearing myself play...twice."

At the completion of the new hall, I thought we had found the perfect way to honor Bobby Kennedy. I went to Ethel Kennedy, RFK's widow, and suggested the new center be named after him and that we use his immortal quotes to adorn the walls. She rejected that idea and said it wasn't good enough. Instead, we named it Smith Hall, dedicated to John F. Kennedy's brother-in-law and advisor, Stephen E. Smith.

When we first started putting on fundraising events for the programs of the Library Foundation, Jackie Kennedy was reluctant to host the dinners and asked me why Caroline couldn't do it.

I told her, "If Caroline hosts, it might sell out, but tickets will go for $150 a pop. If you host, Jackie, we can get $1,500 a plate and everyone will pay."

"Even Ethel?"

"Especially Ethel!"

★ ★ ★

I developed a close relationship with Caroline Kennedy and her husband, Ed Schlossberg, who brought his creative brilliance to a redesign of the museum space and a digitalization of the archives. Caroline was a young mother when she started taking over Jackie's role overseeing the library. Her poise, energy, and charisma were contagious. She was totally dedicated to leading the library, a role her son, Jack, has recently taken up with the same dedication.

JFK Jr. and Caroline Kennedy present me with a watercolor painted by Jackie.

I remember Dick Donahue saying, "I owe all the success in my life to the years I spent working with John F. Kennedy." Working at the library, where Dick remained on the board until his death in 2016, was a way for both of us to carry on our service and to preserve a true account of those special years. The staff I inherited and those I hired were of the same mind. It was about the president's legacy, *not our own.* We worked to avoid hype, faddishness, and over-seriousness. I left the library to a strong succession of federal and foundation directors: John Shattuck, Deborah Leff, Brad Garett, Tom Putnam, and Tom McNaught. These leaders continued to empower the library's public/private partnership that has become the standard for all presidential libraries.

LOVE WALKED IN AND DROVE THE SHADOWS AWAY

1987–

"One look and I had found a world completely new
When love walked in with you."

—GEORGE GERSHWIN

When I came back from Ireland to run the library, I got a lonely room in South Boston. Christine Sullivan was in Boston too, but I didn't want to see her. She didn't know how to share my loss, and I no longer knew how to love anyone. Around New Year's, 1988, I took Christine to dinner at L'Aloutte, a French restaurant on the Cape, to say goodbye. I didn't know how to get over losing Mary. Christine should have moved on. She had loved me for a decade knowing that it would never be possible to be together. Now that it was possible, I was too broken.

Finally, after a time apart that was agonizing for both of us, I realized I couldn't live without her. On the dock of my Cape Cod house, I asked her to marry me. We went for a seafood lunch to celebrate. We set a date for the fall. There was just one issue. She was a Catholic and I'm, at least in theory, a protestant. The first hurdle was visiting her parents on Presentation Road in Brighton.

She told me that I would be the first protestant to set foot on their front porch.

"Not even the mailman?"

"You think a protestant could get a job as a mailman in this neighborhood?"

To this day, she can still tell me the name of the neighborhood mailman, John Kenneally.

With her parents' very warm blessing, we just had the church to worry about. Per Catholic law I had to sign some papers saying I'd raise our children in the church. Signing papers was okay, but on top of that the priest wanted me to go to an adult version of Sunday school. That wasn't going to happen. Fortunately, I had an answer. I knew Father Richard McHugh in Korea, where he had been a Marine lieutenant. He got blown up by a land mine and survived. We saw each other again as guests of Bethesda Naval Hospital. When I left the hospital, he was still undergoing treatment. After the Navy put him back together, McHugh had a spiritual awakening and became a Navy chaplain and went on to serve in Vietnam. I knew he had retired and was living in North Carolina. I called to explain my situation.

"I look forward to seeing you on your knees in front of a Catholic altar," he said.

Father/Lieutenant McHugh married us at Our Lady of the Presentation in Brighton in front of our many friends from the many chapters in our lives.

Christine and I on our wedding day, November 5, 1988.

We honeymooned in the Bahamas followed by Key West, where I introduced Christine to a good friend, Bobby Nesbitt, the piano player The Pier House. When Christine and I walked in the door, Bobby stopped what he was playing and launched into Gershwin's "Love Walked In."

One look and I had found my future at last.

One look and I had found a world completely new.

When love walked in with you.

FIELD WORK

1999–2006

"He resolved to compile his chronicle, so that he should not be one of those who hold their peace but should bear witness in favor of those plague-stricken people; so that some memorial of the injustices and outrage done to them might endure; and to state quite simply what we learn in a time of pestilence: that there are more things to admire in men than to despise."

—ALBERT CAMUS, *THE PLAGUE*

Through our work together in the Ireland Fund, Tony O'Reilly and I built a lasting and trusting friendship. His rugby interested me just as much as the Marine Corps interested him. In our working relationship, mine was often the contrary opinion to the yes-men who told Tony what they thought he wanted to hear. That trust led him to make me a member of the board governing *The Independent,* an Irish newspaper through which he controlled a media empire of 175 news outlets in Ireland, the UK, Australia, New Zealand, India, and South Africa.

In 1999, Tony invited me to join him in Cape Town, where he was meeting with his South Africa Advisory Board. The board reflected the special place Tony had in his heart for a country where, as an eighteen-year-old winger on the Lions, he had played to a packed rugby stadium. Nelson Mandela had attended one of his games, cheering for the foreign team (Tony's) as fans seated in the black section tended to do. Through his business and personal interest in the country, Tony had come to oppose apartheid and went on to help raise money for Nelson Mandela's political work following his quarter century as a political prisoner. *The Independent* had helped lead the way in equal hiring practices by appointing the country's first black editor to one of its papers. The board brought together an impressive international group of politicians, journalists, celebrities, and business leaders to further the dreams of the new, democratic South Africa.

My first trip down there was supposed to be a vacation with Christine.

* * *

As we were landing in Cape Town, I noticed a sea of shacks that I later learned was the township of Khayelitsha, home to many thousands living in poverty and filth alongside the highway leading from the airport to Cape Town, the wealthiest major city in Africa's richest country. I made a mental note of what I had seen from the window of the first-class cabin and resolved to get a closer look at those shacks.

On our limousine ride from the airport to the hotel, the shacks seemed to stretch on endlessly. They were constructed out of sheet metal scraps, street signs, and whatever other materials these poor people could collect.

I asked our driver, a white South African, "Where do these people work?"

"In Cape Town."

"It must be an expensive commute."

"They've got a system: vans, jammed to capacity, each passenger pays a couple of rand for the round trip."

"I assume living in Cape Town is too expensive?"

"That would be true; but even if they did have the money, they wouldn't have been allowed to spend the night in Cape Town under the rules."

The "rules" as in apartheid, which had officially ended just a few years prior. Apartheid literally means "apart."

Not long after we checked in to our elegant room at the Table Bay Hotel, I asked the driver to take me out to Khayelitsha. What I saw there was overwhelming, brutal, and hard to comprehend. There was no basic infrastructure in that shack city, just one or two roads leading to a small shopping center and what appeared to be some sort of clinic.

Before I left the hotel, I had scanned a copy of *The Independent*'s main South African newspaper. There were stories about AIDS with numbers I couldn't fathom. In Khayelitsha, I asked my driver to come back in an hour, not wanting to walk around with a white guy who looked like an ex-cop, which in fact he was. I walked to the clinic.

I introduced myself to a young nurse and asked, "What's this place all about?"

She said a single word, "AIDS."

"Who runs it?"

"Dr. Gomeare."

I asked her to see if he was available.

A middle-aged, simply dressed white man who spoke with a European accent introduced himself as Eric Gomeare and invited me into his office. He told me the clinic is funded by *Médecins Sans Frontières* (MSF), Doctors Without Borders, to address the AIDS epidemic. He explained that so many people die of AIDS in Khayelitsha that funerals are held on Saturdays with twenty minutes allotted to each burial.

"If you want to see more of Khayelitsha, you should have one of my volunteers walk with you. You will be in no danger."

I took him up on the offer and had a look around. I saw single-room shacks with very few windows. The roofs were flimsy and appeared to let in sun and rain. The place stank of shit and garbage and rot. Death hung in the air.

Khayelitsha, South Africa.

After that first visit to the township, I was no longer on holiday. Two days later, I had lunch with Tony. He asked me what I thought of this magnificent country. He was of course referring to the lavish accommodations, the welcoming culture, the wildlife, and the views of Table Mountain towering up into the mist.

I shook my head and gazed out the window at the astonishingly gorgeous view. My mind was in Khayelitsha.

"Tony, this is wonderful. We are very lucky to be here with you...I hate to tell you my impression is that this wonderful place you love so much and the whole dream of a new and fairer South Africa, all of it, all of it, is turning to shit because of AIDS."

He paused. He asked me where I got that opinion in less than forty-eight hours. I told him about Khayelitsha and what the doctor at the clinic had told me. I mentioned that my son, Michael, had written a cover piece for *New York Magazine* back in the 1980s about the AIDS epidemic in America.

"All right," he said, "I want you to join our advisory board. You are hereby appointed *The Independent*'s official advisor on AIDS. We meet every six months. You'll present a report at the next meeting and all future meetings. Tell us what's going on and what you think we can do to be useful."

★ ★ ★

The membership of Tony's South Africa advisory board was impressive. It included Ben Bradlee, who had been executive editor of the *Washington Post* and a hero of Watergate; Shaun Johnson, a South African journalist; former New York Mayor David Dinkins, one of the first black Marines; and Sean Connery, along with three or four members of South African society.

The board would have an annual lunch with Nelson Mandela. At my first meeting with him in South Africa, he noticed my PT-109 tie clip, a souvenir from the Kennedy White House. He told me about his visit to the Kennedy Library. He asked if he could have the tie clip.

"Here it is, but what are you going to do with it? You don't wear a tie."

He clamped the miniature brass boat to his tunic.

Mandela's presence is a staggering and powerful gentleness.

What's truly remarkable about this man is the way his example inspired others to actualize courage and patience in the face of a system that told them they had no dignity and no honor to preserve.

★ ★ ★

Twice every year, I compiled and presented AIDS reports to the advisory board. I tried to convey the problem and to advise how best to use our influence as a foreign-owned media company outside the reach of the denialist government. My goal was to see that our papers did more than bear witness to the tragedy, that we would do everything we could to support those who were helping or trying to help. My AIDS reports were a small part of the advisory board's work. Normally all was lovely and upbeat at these meetings, then it was Daly's turn. Delivering one report, I told the board that my remarks would take twenty-three minutes, one minute for every million lives lost to AIDS to date. That's just twenty-three minutes of a weeklong agenda, a grim footnote to what otherwise tended to be a seminar of optimism.

One of the most immediate and effective things we could do was to make condoms freely available to our employees and promote their use. Leading from the front meant that this practice must start in our own offices, and that I would personally verify the availability of condoms—if not their durability. At one of our papers, I enquired if I could get a condom. They gasped, surprised to hear this from their illustrious visitor from Dublin. They said they didn't have any.

I asked their boss, "Why not?"

On my next visit, they had a bowlful in the pressroom, which they presented with a grin to the old white guy in their midst.

We covered Condom Week, a campaign sponsored by Levi Strauss & Co. reprinting slogans like:

No glove, no love.

Got no protection? Can't use your erection.

Cloak your poker before you poke'r.

Another prevention option is something doctors call "the surgical vaccine." Recent studies showed that circumcision could reduce the instances of sexually transmitted HIV. This is a tricky issue in South Africa because tribal practices vary: some snip, others don't. When Pete McCloskey found out that I was advocating circumcision, it amused him greatly.

"Korea wasn't dangerous enough for him, now he's trying to cut the pricks off Zulu warriors."

In my reports, I would follow bawdy quips with statistics about South Africa's AIDS orphans—850,000 in number as of 2006—and urge anyone who finds boner jokes offensive to consider the obscenity of that number. I swore a lot during the board meetings even by my standards. Some members didn't appreciate my obscene language. I would tell them it's an obscene *fucking* world. Real obscenity is drinking mineral water and vintage wines in a palatial hotel guarded by armed security just a thirty-minute drive from a city of tin shacks where little girls are afraid to use the toilet.

Delivering one of my reports, I paused and choked up, temporarily unable to read the words I had written about a girl, a volunteer at Dr. Gomeare's clinic, whom I had met on earlier visits. This brave and special young woman had been raped and murdered on a trip to the toilet. On December 13, 2003, Lorna Mlofana, an HIV survivor and clinic volunteer, was using the toilet shack when a group of five youths began raping her in turns. In an attempt to deter them, she cried out that she was HIV positive, and for that she was beaten to death by her rapists. Lorna was remembered in a poem that was posted on the door of the clinic where she worked:

So, God, if flowers grow in heaven,

Pick a bunch and put it in her arms and

Tell her it's from the TAC volunteers in Khayelitsha

I put those words in my report, but I couldn't speak them out loud.

One of the most tragic ways HIV was spreading in South Africa was through the breast milk of HIV positive mothers to their unfortunate babies. These transmissions could be easily prevented by cheap drugs (around eighty dollars per patient per year) that were available almost everywhere else in the world. My reports underscored the importance of these drugs and called further attention to the South African government's denialist policies that made it very difficult for patients to get such help. The cost of drugs was a major excuse for anyone trying to justify governmental inaction. This was more bullshit. Other governments worked pharma companies to further lower the cost of these drugs, saving lives at a cost of $3.50 per life per year.

★ ★ ★

Writing these reports involved doing field work in my late seventies. While my status on the board at *The Independent* would get me meetings with heads of government and industry, someone in my position could have just as easily delegated the work of reporting from Khayelitsha to a twenty-three-year-old intern. My aim was to cover and report on the whole problem, from open toilets in the townships, to the offices of corporations, and the halls of government, then *directly* present my findings to persons capable of making a difference. I believed it sent a message to have someone in my position spend time among those shacks.

Remembering our trips to South Africa, Tony told my third son, Charlie, "Chuck went to those damn camps none of us would ever set foot in."

When I returned to Khayelitsha, I was advised to bring a driver (read: armed bodyguard). No way. I would leave my Rolex in the hotel room, keep my gold wedding ring on, and get in a cab that was willing to take me.

I found a place to have a drink in a cinder block building with the word "Bar" painted on the side. The proprietor served through a steel grate from a locked strong room at one end of the bar to protect himself from armed robbery. I shared stories with him about the pubs in Ireland.

At Dr. Gomeare's MSF clinic, I saw volunteers wearing T-shirts printed with the words *HIV Positive*. The story behind these shirts was powerful. Back in 1998, Gugu Dlamini was stoned to death in a Durban township when it became known she had AIDS. Shortly after Dlamini's murder, a friend of hers came out as HIV positive rather than continue to live in fear, waiting to be lynched. She made the T-shirts to break the stigma around the disease, and as a way of saying, "I'm not afraid of you bastards." The shirts became the brand of TAC, the Treatment Action Committee.

It's hard to imagine a place where going to the toilet can be fatal, a place where there's roughly one flush toilet for every seventeen thousand persons, a place that is largely ignored by those with the power to improve those conditions.

In the absence of government leadership on the AIDS issue, rumor and superstition had taken over. One rumor said that condoms had worms in them. A sitting president of South Africa endorsed the rumor that a postcoital shower could prevent AIDS. The Minister of Health went to the World AIDS Conference promoting the rumor that garlic and lemon juice were effective treatments and that HAART (Highly Active Anti-Retroviral Treatment) was more dangerous than AIDS. But the worst rumor of all, the one that once again made me pause to choke back tears at the podium delivering another report, was the rumor that sex with a virgin could cure AIDS. This had sparked an epidemic of infant rape. Researching my report, I sat down with someone whose baby was essentially brain dead following a gang rape. There were instances of four- and five-year-olds who'd already been raped many times. In at least one case, the rapist of a five-year-old was let off on the grounds that his victim was not a virgin.

I don't think anything can prepare someone to understand that kind of suffering. I don't think that kind of suffering can be understood. AIDS in South Africa was death, pointless agony, and cruelty like nothing I had ever seen. These people weren't combatants. They were simply victims of an unlucky birth, even more unlucky than the civilian victims of war. I found their pain to be overwhelming. War may have prepared me to witness such pain without looking away, but nothing could have prepared me to understand it.

My notes didn't change minds or drive legislation, and I didn't even try to convince anyone on the board to come hang out with me at The Bar in Khayelitsha. I was seventy-two years old when I started going to South Africa, and I turned eighty shortly after my final trip. More than once I was asked, "What were you thinking?" Why did I take up field work and reporting in a dangerous place when I could have been golfing and napping? Maybe I had one more battle in me, maybe I don't know how to stay out of it when I see suffering like I found in Khayelitsha. On a personal level, I knew that it felt better to be somewhere I could work with brave and dedicated people whom I admired the way I had admired "Gunner" Dohse and Kenny O'Donnell and finally Dr. Eric Gomeare.

Doctors like Gomeare had risked their medical licenses, their freedom, and even their lives to smuggle in drugs that had been proven to work everywhere but remained unavailable in South Africa. They smuggled in cheap, generic drugs in toys and teddy bears. Eventually they made private contacts at DHL who helped ensure the packages were not too closely scrutinized by customs.

In 2000, Eric's team was expelled from Johannesburg, and they would receive three expulsion orders from Khayelitsha.

"Chuck, you must remember," Eric pointed out, "this is a place where it costs nothing to put a bullet in someone's head."

Whenever I spoke with Eric, he kept it simple for me and always translated statistics and medical jargon into human terms. He told me of one woman who stood up in court, advocating the use of lifesaving drugs, saying, "You don't need a long explanation if you can understand that I am positive, and my baby is negative."

But this man of medicine had no other word but "magic" to describe how HAART works. He spoke of the "Lazarus effect" that happens when someone who has twenty-four hours or less to live comes back from the brink after taking HAART.

"Chuck, being surrounded with these sorts of survivors...these things carry you for the rest of your life."

In 2002, Eric had another experience that would buoy him through several more years of denial and obstruction: Mandela paid a visit to his clinic. He put on an *HIV Positive* T-shirt over his tunic and declared, "We must manage this disease, or it will manage us."

Eric implored him, "Please come to our rescue."

To me, Eric's words were an uncanny reminder of the appeal to my doctor-grandfather from a plague-stricken provincial hospital in China: *For God's sake come to me, Daly, we are dying.*

At the time of Mandela's visit, there were four million South Africans living with HIV/AIDS, and not one on HAART in the public sector.

At one of the advisory board's lunches with Nelson Mandela, he told us that he believed the greatest failure of his life was not taking decisive action on AIDS and that he didn't grasp the urgency of the problem until it took the life of his nephew.

Another milestone was marked by Judge Cameron, a high court

judge with white skin, who came out as HIV positive stating publicly that the only reason he was alive was his private access to HAART and the money to pay for it.

Judge Cameron once told me, "Just being alive causes me shame."

When Eric and his team decided to bring drugs into the country openly, they called the press, and our papers championed the cause. Thereafter, three million South Africans threatened to go on strike if the doctors were arrested.

In 2008, the South African government finally sat down with TAC activists. At the 2010 World AIDS Conference, the new health minister, Dr. Aaron Motsoaledi, said, "Today we are guided by science."

TAC took an active role in shaping new government policies. Still, an estimated 356,000 South Africans would have lived were it not for Mbeki's policies.[29]

Eric still works in South Africa. He was in Khayelitsha when Charlie called to interview him for this book. The woman from the head office of MSF in South Africa who got me contact info said the name "Eric" with the inflection of hope and awe with which I heard others say "Bobby" a long time ago.

A few years back, Eric had been given a new post as general director for MSF's Operational Center in Brussels.

"But it wasn't my turf," he said.

---

29 Celia W. Dugger, "Study Cites Toll of AIDS Policy in South Africa," *New York Times*, November 25, 2008.

He requested and was approved to return to field work in Khayelitsha.

★ ★ ★

In the middle of delivering one of my final AIDS reports, I started mumbling. That was nothing new, I mumble all the time. As my fellow board member, Lady Margaret Jay, remembers, "I'd have liked to have understood more of what he said, because it all seemed interesting."

The problem that day was that I don't remember mumbling. I don't remember halting my report in midsentence. I don't remember returning to my seat at the board table. After several minutes I could not account for, I asked David Dinkins, who was sitting next to me, what had happened.

"You just stopped. Are you okay?"

"I think so."

★ ★ ★

After the meeting, I contacted Margaret Jay's husband, Dr. Michael Adler. He surmised that I'd had a minor stroke, the good kind of stroke if there is such a thing. He told me to get to a hospital right away. I found all this more than a little upsetting. I wanted to get back to Christine and the boys at once. So I did what was apparently one of the worst things imaginable for a stroke survivor: I hopped on a series of flights lasting twenty-four hours.

A doctor in the States scolded me for flying and told me I was lucky to be alive. He ran tests, wrote prescriptions, and recommended that I stay away from the three great pleasures of my old age: tennis, red wine, and Viagra. Hearing the doctor's advice, I was transported back to 1942. I remembered sitting in a waiting room at Johns Hopkins University Hospital in Baltimore. I could hear my father's voice through the door to the doctor's office after he had just been told that the best he could do to live with multiple sclerosis was cut out martinis, golf, and his pipe. I will never forget his response: "Do you expect me to live in a vacuum tube?"

"Have a nice day, Doctor," I said and walked out the door, into Christine's arms.

EPILOGUE

2020

"Summer Grasses,
All that remains
of warriors' dreams."

—HAIKU BY MATSUO BASHŌ

I started working on this book the day after President Kennedy was murdered. I jotted and typed my thoughts and observations on four-by-six index cards, which I tossed in a box and forgot about when I left the White House. Since then, friends and family have told me I should write a book. A journalist recently told Christine, "Chuck *has to* talk one of these days" ...whatever that means. It wasn't 'til after my ninetieth birthday, I began writing again. I started with what I *could* talk about, stories my family already knew. When it came to war, I froze. I didn't know how to write about what it was really like. I had no words for my most vivid memories, and I refused to create a polite version of what it was like or spin some "hoorah!" fairy tale. The original purpose of this book was to leave a record of my life for my family. What would they think about my having committed a war crime? Was it unfair to put the images in their heads that I couldn't get out of mine?

I once told a friend, Bob Manning, former editor of the *Atlantic*, who was writing his own memoir, "If you can't tell the truth, don't write the book."

It was time for me to take my own advice. I approached my son, Charlie, about collaborating on this project. He suggested we start by just talking through my notes and expanding those conversations into the prose of a memoir. With my family's support and encouragement, I gradually started talking about the things I *couldn't* talk about. It wasn't easy. There were days when we would talk for ten minutes and I'd break down and go on a long walk. Other times, it was the opposite, he couldn't get me to shut up or to slow down so he could take notes.

Charlie supplemented our conversations with background research and hours of interviews with friends, family, and colleagues. His interview notes ran over a thousand pages. Through an obscure local newspaper in Canada, he got in touch with the Royal Canadian Legion Hall in Whitecourt, Alberta, David Ivens's hometown. He started emailing with Kyle Scott, a sapper in the Canadian army, veteran of the war in Afghanistan, and president of the Whitecourt Legion Hall. He told us that Ivens's mother spent the rest of her life petitioning the Legion to add David's name to their cenotaph as an exception to the rule that those memorialized must have died serving in Canadian or Commonwealth forces. She got her wish. David's name is there now on the wall of the Legion Hall of the snowmobile capital of Canada. Scott's own research revealed that besides serving heroically in WWII with Canadian forces, Ivens had the longest disciplinary record of anyone he'd ever seen.

Charlie also managed to track down Billy Bell. The woman at the VFW hall in his hometown in Arizona said that his favorite war story was the one about the lieutenant who said, "I hope you're left handed" after his right arm was blown off. He's in a VA nursing home now, where I'm assured they're taking good care of him. I called to double-check. He had been a teacher, a husband, and is described as "a pillar of the community."

I didn't always see the point in putting my memories on the page, but little by little, I could see that the process was helping me make peace with my life. My great fear in publishing these words is that I'm somehow trading on the bodies of the men who didn't come home. My great hope is that I may help someone by showing them it's possible to have a useful life with a disabled body and a wounded mind.

★ ★ ★

In the summer of 2019, I sat down with retired Navy SEAL and bestselling author Jocko Willink, as a guest on his podcast. He read from my manuscript and we talked about my life and about war. A chilling moment was when he read the line about the time I asked my father when the memories of war will fade.

I said that they don't fade.

Jocko replied, "No, they don't."

Recording *Jocko Podcast*, Episode 196.

I spent a long time preparing for the podcast to avoid rambling or choking up, which I did anyway. Nothing could have prepared me for the response from his listeners. The podcast was accessed over fifty thousand times on YouTube. Hundreds of comments came in from all over the world. Listeners emailed, they Tweeted. The deputy chief of our local police department, where Jocko's *Extreme Ownership* is required reading, came to my door one day to shake my hand and give me a mug with the department crest on it. I was astonished by how many young people are interested in the history of the Korean War. *They* haven't forgotten. One listener, a Korean Marine, thanked me for saving his country.

Another listener wrote: "My father was in the Korean War and he never talked about it. Now I know why."

★ ★ ★

Trying to fit my life into a book meant cutting out and glossing over some people and events that meant more to me than the space they take up in these pages might suggest. Most notably, my family.

My first son, Michael, was a columnist for the *New York Daily News*, where he worked with my old pal, Jimmy Breslin. Over the years, Michael's writing focused on New York firefighters and cops. Some of his closest friends were the men he wrote about, and many of them died on September 11. His book *The Book of Mychal* tells the story of the FDNY chaplain, a close friend of his, who was the first official victim at the World Trade Center. His heartrending columns about that day and its aftermath earned him consideration for a Pulitzer. He came in second to a *New York Times* columnist.

Douglas was drawn to science from a young age and started work as a botanist in the Amazon shortly after he finished university. His work took him to the rainforest in Colombia at a time when guerillas and narco-terrorists made that a very dangerous place to be. I once told him how much it would upset his mother should anything happen to him.

"Dad," he replied, "the rainforest is my Marine Corps. But I'll never have to kill anyone."

He's now the New York Botanical Gardens' Curator of Amazonian Botany.

We built a living memorial to Mary with the Mary Daly Fund, which was managed by our family and Mary's friends in Bantry, Ireland, for the purpose of helping cultural and social causes in the town and surrounding West Cork. The Fund lasted thirty years. In 2017 we gave our final and largest grant, $100,000, to West Cork Women Against Violence. A cause that was close to

Mary and later Christine as they made friends with women in Bantry—wives of pillars of the community in some cases—who had been victims of domestic violence and of the culture of silence that enabled it.

* * *

I became a father again, at sixty-two, when Christine and I welcomed Charlie into the world. He had a rough arrival, spending the first week of his life on a breathing tube, chances of survival uncertain at best. Of my four sons (Michael, Douglas, Charlie, and Kevin), he seems to have inherited the most acute case of restlessness. A kayaker, bodysurfer, and free diver, his lifelong love of the ocean began on the shore in front of our summer home in Bantry Bay. Freelance writing has given him a way to be professionally curious and throw his energy into a half-dozen interesting projects at once. He lives in Europe. This will be his first book. He's currently at work on his second and third.

My youngest, Kevin, is wrapping up his twenties having squeezed an extraordinary amount of life into his first decade of adulthood. He's led the Yale rugby team as their captain, the GOAT (greatest of all time) according to my research, though he denies this. He worked on the Deal Team at Blackstone before deciding to go to law school. He's now at Penn Law in their JD/MBA program with Wharton, combining business and law. I know I won't be around to see what he does with that education, but I'm in awe of what I've seen so far, and I'm lucky to have seen this much.

Both Kevin and Christine were indispensable to this memoir as editors and tiebreakers when Charlie and I were at a stalemate over a word choice or some such thing. It was Christine who discovered the box of index card notes from the early days of the Johnson administration.

On Cape Cod with Christine, Summer, 2019 (Photo/Katherine Brackman).

I carried on as a board member at the American Ireland Fund until 2015. I finally retired completely in 2019, when I left the board of the Joyce Foundation. At my retirement party, I was

given a letter from President Barack Obama, with whom I had
served on that board, back when he was an Illinois State Senator.

The Joyce Foundation board. Dick Donahue is second to the right in the back.

He wrote, "From your service and sacrifice in defending the
values that define who we are as a nation to your dogged devotion to clearing the pathways to opportunity for our young people,
it is in your example that we see the true meaning of patriotism
and of nobility."

★ ★ ★

As this book goes to print, I only wish some of the topics weren't
so relevant to current events. All my meetings with the publishing
team and editors have been remote, over video conference calls,
as Christine and I practice social distancing on Cape Cod. The
denial and inaction I'm seeing at the highest levels of government
in this country remind me of the denialist, anti-science govern-

ments in South Africa. The results are frustratingly, tragically the same: pointless, preventable death, and idiotic conspiracy theories that compound the suffering.

Riots are once again tearing America apart, just as they were when I was at the University of Chicago in 1968. Now, as then, I'm sympathetic to the protesters' anger over Vietnam then and racial injustice now. I see civil disobedience and free speech as the highest duties of patriotism, but I've seen enough violence to know that it's a dead end—literally. I'm reminded of Bobby Kennedy's improvised remarks upon learning of Martin Luther King Jr.'s assassination:

> "What we need in the United States is not division; what we need in the United States is not hatred; what we need in the United States is not violence or lawlessness; but love and wisdom, and compassion toward one another, and a feeling of justice toward those who still suffer within our country, whether they be white or they be black."

Korea is still divided and still a potential powder keg. There are still land mines in the hills, even in the South. What little we know about the hell that is North Korea gives us a glimpse at what might have become of the whole peninsula if my brothers and I hadn't held the line!

While we were working to get the manuscript ready, my editor told me that people don't read memoirs to learn about the author, they read them to learn about themselves. I hope you've learned something. I have no advice, but I'll leave you with a question asked of me on my first day at work in the White House,

> "What have you done for your country lately?"

ACKNOWLEDGMENTS

First, I want to thank Christine for her help and support, even with the parts that must have been hard for her to read, and for always kicking my ass to keep going. My sons: Michael, who gave us the nudge we needed to get started on this project; Kevin, our patient editor; Douglas, our expert source on Irish history and the only Daly who speaks the Irish language; his wife, Gloria, who helped source dozens of family photos. And Charlie, my writing partner. My grandchildren, Bronagh, Aiden, and Sinéad, who is the keeper of the telegram I received in Korea announcing her father's birth. My sisters, Joan Hicks and Anne Daly Goodwin. My niece, Sealey-King Gilles, who helped with the photos and family history. My brother-in-law, Kevin Sullivan, who provided Unruh family history from his days in the unions in California. Roger Sullivan. LCDR Brendan Sullivan, USCG, our active duty military fact-checker and his wife, Lauren, Meghan Sullivan and Jasmine Sullivan Waits, who confirmed that we picked the right title. And Oonagh Paulson.

My friends: Pete McCloskey and his wife, Helen; Gunther Dohse; Angus and Madlyn Deming; Helen Aylmer. Major General Michael Lehnert. Michael Claffey and Betsy Hearne for so many unforgettable dinners on both sides of the Atlantic, for editing and insights. Nancy Donahue, for decades of friendship and helping me write about what it was like to be married to the West Wing. Philip Donahue, "I love you too!" Sir Anthony O'Reilly, who trusted me to tell the truth, even when he didn't want to hear it.

Jocko Willink for inviting me on his podcast and for all he does to honor our veterans and remember the fallen. His listeners showed me that young people haven't "forgotten" the Korean War.

Steven Pressfield, this all started with a single page on a legal pad. Semper fi!

The Scribe team for helping me cross the finish line with this book.

The staff at the JFK Library: Shelly Sommer, Donna Smerlas, Frank Rigg, Maura Porter, Tom Putnam, Rachel Day Flor, Karren Mullen, Amy McDonald, Amy Foreman, Doris Drummond, Maura Hammer, and the heroic and moral Sam Rubin.

The Joyce Foundation board and staff: Michael Brewer, Jose Alvarez, Carlton Guthrie, Deborah Gillespie, Ellen Alberding, Jack Anderson, Sally Wilkins, and Linda Schelinski Joyce.

Tracie Shea, devoted to mending minds, who read early drafts for insights into PTSD. Tom McNaught, fact-checker, researcher, guide, and above all, beloved friend. Matthew Gilbert for his early advice and mentorship, for helping us believe this was a worthwhile project. Sally Jackson for helping us cut through the bullshit and connect with our audience. David Goodwillie, another mentor in the writing craft and the book game. Sterling Lord, my agent from back in the Columbia J-school days, hanging in there at ninety-nine.

Our early readers and advice-givers: Sharon King Hoge, Jon Low, Aodhán Hurley, Kate Driscoll, Lew Butler, Joe Toomey, Maureen Lechwar, Frank Connors and Martha Meaney, Liz Wellington, Eleanore Dunfey-Freiburger, Jim Rowe, Mary Gaule, Dominique Müller, Thomas P. O'Neill III, and Colin Macguire, "you saved the day," semper fi!

Dr. Briscoe, who saved Charlie's life. Dr. Sam Decker and Dr. Sophie-Virginie Honecker for explaining the medical complexity of my wounded arm. The "meatball surgeons," corpsmen, and Navy doctors; without their skill, I'd have written this book with one arm. Dr. Casey Sweeney, Cpt. USMCR, Richard "Drew" Marcantonio, and Frank Manaloto, semper fi! C-1-5, "Make peace or die!" CPL Kyle Scott, Canadian Army; Chimo! Sappers lead the way. Bobby Nesbit, who sang Cole Porter over the phone to Charlie when he interviewed him for the book. Deannie McDonnel, Tom Kelly, Shirley Kelly, Mike U. and Cory W., Margaret Jay and Dr. Michael Adler, Dave Denelo, Kenny O'Donnell Jr., Paul and Gail Kirk, Bill McNally, Dr. Eric Gomeare, Judy Hayes, Jackie Redpath and the Greater Shankill Partnership, Michael Burke, Sean and Teressa O'Luasa, Cricket Redmond Kerrebock, Gary Hymel, Mary Pearl, Meredith Ashley, Alexis Dacy, Ted Barker.

ABOUT THE AUTHORS

CHARLES U. DALY

Charles U. Daly is the last living member of John F. Kennedy's West Wing congressional liaison staff. Before that, he led a Marine rifle platoon through some of the most intense combat of the Korean war and was awarded a Silver Star and a Purple Heart. He helped run several American institutions, including the University of Chicago, Harvard, and the JFK Presidential Library. He has four sons, ages 28 to 69, and lives on Cape Cod with his wife, Christine. He attributes his long life to tennis, red wine, and Viagra.

CHARLIE DALY

Charlie Daly is a freelance writer. He worked on this book as his father's writing partner. These pages are but a small excerpt from their many tearful and joyous conversations.